# SAVARKAR and HINDUTVA

# SAVARKAR and HINDUTVA

## The Godse Connection

A.G. Noorani

LeftWord

First published November 2002.
Reprinted June 2003, January 2004, September 2005,
March 2009, August 2011, September 2015, November 2017
Digital print edition, March 2020

LeftWord Books
2254/2A Shadi Khampur
New Ranjit Nagar
New Delhi 110008
India
www.leftword.com

LeftWord Books is a division of
Naya Rasta Publishers Pvt. Ltd.



ISBN 978-81-87496-83-0

TO THE VICTIMS OF
THE POGROM IN GUJARAT 2002
AND TO THE MEDIA, PRINT AND ELECTRONIC,
WHICH DID INDIA PROUD

# CONTENTS

# PREFACE

Believers in the ideology of Hindutva are in the driving seat of power in India today. Though its author, Vinayak Damodar Savarkar, was at pains to emphasize that he had 'coined' the term in 1923 for the theme of his essay *Hindutva*, many persist in identifying it with Hinduism. Neither Swami Vivekananda nor Swami Rama Tirth nor, for that matter, any of the other great exponents of this noble faith used the word Hindutva. That Hindutva is a political philosophy that has nothing to do with religion is also seen in the fact that its author Savarakar himself was an atheist, and had little time for religion or philosophy. He was engaged in a political enterprise, and used history in the service of his politics of hate.

In 1989–90, the BJP adopted the credo of Hindutva. Only in 2002 could Lal Kishen Advani, the BJP's foremost exponent of Hindutva, muster courage to laud Savarkar as a national hero. It is a sinister move whose implications will emerge only gradually, as did the impact of Hindutva in the last decade since the BJP began advocating it openly. It is a blood-soaked trail, from the demolition of the Babri Masjid, on December 6, 1992, right down to the pogrom in Gujarat in 2002. The BJP has profited by its Ayodhya campaign, as Advani has acknowledged time and again. The nation suffered grievously and wantonly. There was no other way that the RSS political front could have won power.

Savarkar had pitted himself against the ideology of Indian nationalism. He rejected the concept of 'territorial nationalism' and advocated the concept of 'cultural nationalism'. The RSS and the BJP swear by it. The content and contours of Hindutva emerge sharply from the writings of Savarkar and of the leaders of the RSS and the BJP.

The BJP's attempt to project Savarkar as a national hero is, in effect, as attempt to displace Gandhi from his position as a symbol of Indian nationalism. That Vallabhbhai Patel and a Commission of Inquiry headed by Justice Jivan Lal Kapur, a former judge of the Supreme Court of India, held that Savarkar led the conspiracy to kill Gandhi makes the BJP's game all the more insidious and revolting. Its object is to recast India's polity and reshape its ethos. Saffronization of education is a part of that wider aim. Savarkar is lauded as a hero despite his repeated and abject apologies to the British rulers and his offers to collaborate with them against the Congress. Every archival disclosure shows him in a poor light. Shyama Prasad Mookerjee –founder of the Jan Sangh, and in a sense, the BJP as well – was very much privy to this in 1942 a propos the Quit India Movement. It was the British who spurned his offer.

One had read accounts of Savarkar's role in Gandhi's murder and of his politics. Advani's move to install him on the pedestal prompted this writer to collect the material and submit it to the judgement of fellow citizens. We face a serious menace.

I wish to record my thanks to Prof. Mushirul Hasan, Director, Third World Studies, Jamia Milia Islamia, New Delhi for help in the research and Shilpi Goswami at LeftWord Books for her pains over the manuscript. Sudhanva Deshpande, Managing Editor, LeftWord Books, went beyond his usual help which has always been enormous. This time, apart from editing the manuscript, he assisted in the research as well. Nor must I forget his other colleagues at this remarkable publishing house. None of these friends is responsible for the contents of this book, for which the author alone is responsible.

Last, but not the least, I must acknowledge the invaluable help, rendered over more than a decade-and-a-half, by P.M. Mathews and make amends for my remissness in the past. He is the one who deciphers my scribblings and puts them into legible scripts in typescripts. That holds good for the books as well as articles that I have written since 1985.

I owe him an enormous debt.

*Mumbai* A.G. Noorani

# 1 THE MYTH AND THE MAN

THOUGH DELAYED, JUSTICE has finally been done to the man.

By publicly and explicitly owning up Vinayak Damodar Savarkar as its hero and cult figure, the Bharatiya Janata Party (BJP) finally nailed its colours firmly to the mast of Savarkarism on May 4, 2002. This was a somewhat belated acknowledgement of the party's enormous ideological debt to him. His name was not invoked even when, over a decade ago, Lal Kishan Advani, then BJP's Prime Minister-in-waiting, hitched his party's political fortunes to the star of Hindutva. This term, 'Hindutva', is of relatively recent vintage. It was *coined* in 1923 by Savarkar, who repeatedly made it plain that the term was *not to be confused with Hinduism.* The BJP's apparent neglect of its hero was gross and seemed inexplicable. It was almost as if, to draw an analogy, the Communist movement had forsworn the very mention of the name of Karl Marx. The BJP's omission, however, is perfectly understandable when one recalls the party's style of shaping and re-shaping its public image in order to cover up its real commitment and its true faith, ever since it was established in 1980.

It is difficult to imagine Advani saying, even as late as 1989, what he said at Port Blair on May 4, 2002. He was there to rename Port Blair airport in the Andaman Islands as Veer Savarkar Airport. *The Times of India* tells us that 'Advani dwelt at length on how he idolized Savarkar *from* [sic] *his youth* after he read his book *The First War of Independence* [sic] in 1942. . . . He confessed that it was in *Savarkar's writings* that he had come across the "*much maligned word Hindutva*".'[1] Quite right, for he could not have found the term in the writings of Vivekananda or Aurobindo Ghose. They preached the noble philosophy of Hinduism. Savarkar, on the other hand, coined the term in his essay *Hindutva: Who is a Hindu?* (1923), to propagate the two-nation theory and a cult of hate. Hinduism is noble and ancient. It shows man the path to self-realization. Hindutva, on the other hand, is modern and ignoble. It debases man by arousing his basest emotions – fear and hatred.

The term 'Hindutva' does not occur in Savarkar's book *The First Indian War of Independence – 1857* published in 1909. Therefore, prime among 'Savarkar's writings' on which Advani drew was *Hindutva*, followed by a considerable body of writings and speeches. That Advani drank deep at the fount of Hindutva became clear when he began propagating Hindutva as he embarked on his Rath Yatra ('Chariot Procession', for the construction of a Ram temple at Ayodhya) on September 25, 1990. *Yet, its authorship was not acknowledged* – that was done only at Port Blair. 'There is no reason to fight shy of . . . Hindutva, propounded at great length by Veer Savarkar. It's an all-encompassing ideology with its roots in the country's heritage'.[2] Why, then, the reticence in acknowledging this earlier?

## Savarkar and Gandhi

The renaming of Port Blair airport was incidental to Advani's real mission. He sought to use the occasion to send a message which was not lost on observers: 'Home Minister L.K. Advani sent out a signal that neither he nor his party was apologetic about their Hindutva ideology'. Advani said, "Today, Hindutva is considered an offensive word. But we must remember that the pioneers of Hindutva like Veer Savarkar and RSS founder Hedgewar kindled fierce, nationalistic spirit that contributed to India's liberation".'[3]

This is a brazen falsehood. Savarkar met the arch imperialist Viceroy of India, Lord Linlithgow, in Bombay on October 9, 1939 – the month Congress asked its ministers in the Provinces to resign – and pledged his enthusiastic co-operation to the British. Linlithgow reported to Lord Zetland, the Secretary of State for India:

> The situation, he [Savarkar] said, was that His Majesty's Government must now turn to the Hindus and work with their support. After all, though we and the Hindus have had a good deal of difficulty with one another in the past, that was equally true of the relations between Great Britain and the French and, as recent events had shown, of relations between Russia and Germany. *Our interests were now the same and we must therefore work together.* Even though now the most moderate of men, he had himself been in the past an adherent of a revolutionary party, as possibly, I might be aware. (I confirmed that I was.) But now that our interests were so closely bound together the essential thing was for Hinduism and Great Britain to be friends, and the old antagonism was no longer necessary.[4]

The 'fierce nationalistic spirit' that Savarkar kindled was the spirit of *Hindu* nationalism, *not* Indian nationalism. Advani visited Savarkar's cell in the Cellular Jail Complex. 'Though the Morarji Desai government [of the Janata Party of which Advani and Atal Behari Vajpayee were members between 1977–79] declared the entire complex a national memorial in February 1979, a plaque was *recently* put up in Savarkar's cell, which hailed him as a leader who gave the country the "mantra of Hindutva, equality among Hindus, *Hindu nationhood*, Akhand Bharat".'[5] No reference to *Indian* nationalism.

It is notable, too, that Morarji Desai studiously refrained from honouring Savarkar in 1979. Morarji Desai, of course, was no acolyte of Jawaharlal Nehru at whom Advani took wide swipes at Port Blair. As Home Minister of Bombay Province, Desai had assigned its celebrated Advocate-General C.K. Daphtary to the prosecution, *inter alios*, of Savarkar in the Gandhi murder conspiracy case. The investigation was conducted by his trusted, hand-picked police officer, Jamshid ('Jimmy') D. Nagarwala, Deputy Commissioner of Police in charge of the Bombay CID Special Branch's Sections One and Two. He was responsible for the gathering of local political intelligence.

Savarkar escaped conviction in the case by the skin of his teeth. The law requires that the evidence of an accomplice to a crime must be corroborated in all material respects by independent evidence. Savarkar was acquitted only because the approver Digamber Badge's evidence, which damned Savarkar, did not have independent corroboration as the law requires. But Judge Atma Charan accepted Badge as a truthful witness. 'He gave his version of the facts in a direct and straight-forward manner. He did not evade cross-examination or attempt to evade or fence with any question.' His version was that on January 17, he went with the assassin, Nathuram Vinayak Godse, and accomplice Narayan Apte to Savarkar's home and that he heard Savarkar, while bidding them farewell, say: '*Yashasvi houn ya*' (Be successful and come back). On the way back, Apte told Badge that Savarkar had predicted that 'Gandhiji's 100 years were over – there was no doubt that that work would be successfully finished.'[6]

Nathuram Godse hailed Savarkar in the court as the 'most faithful advocate of the Hindu cause.' The two had known each other since 1929. Therefore, it was natural that Savarkar came under a heavy cloud of suspicion immediately on Gandhi's assassination at the Birla House in New Delhi on January 30, 1948. His house was searched by the police the very next day and a watch was kept at it. He was arrested on February 5, and put in prison. On March 11, while in prison, he was served with a warrant of arrest issued by the Presidency Magistrate in Delhi. The charge was participation in a conspiracy to kill Gandhi, the man he loathed most.

In his famous speech at the All India Congress Committee on August 8, 1942, shortly before it passed the Quit India resolution, Gandhi said: 'Those Hindus who, like Dr Moonje and Shri Savarkar, believe in the doctrine of the sword may seek to keep the Mussalmans under Hindu domination. I do not represent that section. I represent the Congress.'[7] Gandhi and Savarkar represented two diametrically opposite outlooks. The ideologies and policies they represented clashed sharply. Gandhi championed Indian nationalism. Savarkar rejected the very concept of Indian nationalism.

Naturally, therefore, Savarkar rejected India's National Flag adopted by the Constituent Assembly of India on July 22, 1947. This flag was adopted unanimously, 'the whole Assembly standing'.[8] Sarojini Naidu, the last speaker in the discussion, said in a moving peroration, 'Whether we be Hindus or Muslims, Christians, Jains, Sikhs or Zoroastrians and others, our Mother India has one undivided heart and one indivisible spirit. Men and women of reborn India, rise and salute this Flag. I bid you, rise and salute the Flag. (Loud cheers).' The President of the Assembly, Dr Rajendra Prasad, sensing the unanimity, said 'I would ask Members to express their assent to the Resolution which has show their respect to the Flag by getting up and standing in their places for half a minute'.

A week later, on July 29, Savarkar issued a statement in which, sneering at Gandhi, he welcomed the replacement of the *charkha* (spinning wheel) by the *chakra* (wheel) from the Ashoka Pillar at Sarnath. 'This old attitude of the Congressites provoked naturally a sturdy opposition which, led by the Hindu Sanghatanists in particular, had at last succeeded in getting the symbol Charkha removed and relegated to its proper sphere – the Khadi Bhandar [Khadi Store], where it may fittingly serve as a trade mark of any spinning association.' He added,

> Having thus noted impartially the good points in the new Flag adopted for the Indian Union which render it much less objectionable, I must emphatically state it can never be recognized as the National Flag of Hindusthan. Firstly, because the state of Indian Union and the so-called Constituent Assembly are the creation of the British will and not of the free choice of our people ascertained by a national plebiscite and their ultimate sanction even today is the British bayonet and not the national consent or national strength. Secondly, the very mention of the Indian Union reminds us of the break-up of the unity of India as a nation and a state, the vivisection of our Motherland, and the treacherous Congressite abetment of the crime. How can a genuine nationalist salute such a Flag adopted by such a party with no mandate from the nation as a National Flag!

> No: The authoritative Flag of Hindusthan, our Motherland and Holyland, undivided and indivisible from the Indus to the Seas, can be no other than the Bhagava [saffron flag] with the Kundalini and the Kripan inscribed on it to deliver expressly the message of the very Being of our Race! It is not made to order but it is self-evolved with the evolution of our National Being. It mirrors the whole panorama of our Hindu History, is actually worshipped by millions of millions of Hindus and is already flying from the summits of the Himalayas to the Southern Seas. Other Party Flags will be tolerated, some may even by respected in corresponding courtesy but *Hindudom at any rate can loyally salute no other Flag but this Pan-Hindu Dhwaja, this Bhagava Flag as its national Standard.*[9]

This is, of course, of a piece with the recently unveiled plaque in Savarkar's cell in the prison at Port Blair. This is the man the BJP hails as a national hero. *Coming as it does close on the heels of the Gujarat pogrom, Advani's extravagant praise for Savarkar therefore marks a defining moment in the history of the BJP.* Advani has, of course, set his sights the office of Prime Minister of India which he hopes to occupy after the General Elections due in 2004, if not earlier. But his larger aim is more far-reaching than that. He wants the BJP to shed all inhibitions, forced on the party by the constraints imposed by sheer circumstance, and come out boldly, openly with an alternative credo of its own – the credo of Hindutva. He would then proclaim its author Savarkar as a national hero to replace Gandhi. Advani bitterly lamented at Port Blair that 'some parties, because of their narrow ideological philosophy [sic] made the heroes of freedom struggle a preserve of a particular political organization or a family!'[10] The reference here is, of course, to the Indian National Congress. Socialists and Communists were among its proud members. So were members of the Hindu Mahasabha until 1938 when the Congress forbade dual membership with communal bodies. The Mahasabha collaborated with the British while Congressmen went to prison in the struggle for freedom. The Congress stood for Indian nationalism. Savarkar propounded the slogan: 'Hinduize politics and militarize

Hindudom'. Advani and other admirers of Savarkar complain that their hero 'did not get his due'. But saying this is to invite attention to Savarkar's and his admirers' record of patriotism and sacrifice. And such a course, as we shall see, is fraught with risk. The risk of the truth coming out in the open.

### Embracing Hindutva

The mouthpiece of the RSS, *The Organiser*, reported that on March 13, 1991, 'a galaxy of leaders and intellectuals remembered Savarkar on a "never before scale".'[11] The 'galaxy' comprised, among others, of L.K. Advani, M.L. Sondhi, Ram Jethmalani, V.K. Malhotra, Vijaya Raje Scindia, and Balarao Savarkar. The report summed up Advani's contribution in a sentence: 'Advaniji described his writing power [sic] and patriotism.' It will be recalled that at Port Blair, Advani had claimed that he had 'idolized Savarkar from his youth'. But the 1991 report makes no mention of it. The idolization was evidently hermetically sealed in his bosom, for disclosure at a convenient moment.

This belated 'justice' to Savarkar is typical of the stealth and deceit by which the BJP has been advancing towards its goal of Hindu Rashtra as advocated by its mentor, the RSS, as well as its hero, Savarkar.[12]

When the Jan Sangh members of the Janata Party resigned in April 1980 on the issue of their dual membership of the RSS, there was but one honest course before them: revive the Jan Sangh. They did not, because they knew its name was mud. They chose, instead, to sail under the false colours of the Janata Party founded by Jayaprakash Narayan. Five years later, at Bhopal on July 20, 1985, Vajpayee denied that there was any crisis of identity: 'when did we get away from the Jan Sangh?', he asked rhetorically.[13]

However, only five years ago, in a revealing interview to *Debonair*, Vajpayee had said that the BJP was 'different' from the Jan Sangh:

> The Jan Sangh was functioning more or less as an opposition group . . . *with a Hindu bias*. Nothing wrong in that because

> the legitimate interests of all sections of the Indian society are to be preserved and promoted. But the JS got a certain image. Because it was founded in 1951, because Dr Mookerjee was its founder, because immediately after the [P]artition we took up the abolition of article 370 [of the Constitution, conferring special status on Kashmir].

One factor was 'the connection with the RSS to some extent'. The magazine asked the obvious question:

> *Debonair*: Gandhiji's murder?
> *Vajpayee*: Yes, all that old background.

When asked, 'To what extent are you more acceptable to the minorities?' Vajpayee replied: 'It is not a question of being more acceptable to the minorities. It is a question of being more acceptable to the majority'.[14] Like the Jan Sangh, the BJP was out to woo the Hindu vote. If Hindutva and Savarkar were not mentioned, one reason was 'Gandhiji's murder' and 'all that old background', S.P. Mookerjee included.

Mark the landmarks on the route of the rake's progress. The BJP's first plenary convention in Mumbai on December 28, 1980 declared 'Gandhian socialism' to be one of its five commitments along with 'positive secularism' and value-based politics. Hindutva did not figure in the discourse. In 1985 the BJP's National Executive abandoned 'Gandhian Socialism'. The National Council restored it but combined it with the Jan Sangh President Deen Dayal Upadhyaya's 'Integral Humanism'. Even its Palampur Resolution of June 11, 1989 on the Babri Masjid did not mention Hindutva. Advani said on September 24, 1990, the day before he launched his Rath Yatra from the Somnath temple to Ayodhya: 'Ideologically, I am ranged against all the political parties because of this issue. All political parties think alike.' The issue was clearly defined. It was not the Ram Janmabhoomi issue. It was '*a crusade in defence of Hindutva* and a crusade against pseudo secularism.' Its goal was to break from the Gandhi-Nehru ethos, itself a culmination of the Congress ideology since its birth in 1885, and to evolve an alternative ethos.

Even so, neither the 1989 nor the 1991 Election Manifesto of the BJP mentioned Hindutva. That was done first in 1996 and again in 1998. And its author Savarkar was lauded only in 2002. Now that Savarkar has finally come to the fore, can his acolyte Nathuram Vinayak Godse – Gandhi's assassin – be very far behind? When will the Sangh *parivar* (family) laud *him*? When it has established Hindu Rashtra? This is not as implausible as it may appear. *The Hindu* reported that 'Britain's Sangh Parivar celebrated India's Independence Day today by resolving to "advocate Godse's outlook and action" and challenge every anti-national Mulla-Commie', a short hand for Muslims and Communists.[15] In an email to *parivar* members, Bipin Patel, a hard-core Hindutva activist *and believed to close to the Deputy Prime Minister, L.K. Advani,* warned that 'every drop of blood needs to be avenged. And we are ready at any cost.' It added 'we see the merit in Gandhi's [sic] but only after all theology inspired terrorists are *reduced to dead meat.* Till that goal is not achieved, we *advocate Godse's outlook and action.* And if in the meantime, a Gandhi comes to create hurdles in the way, then that Gandhi would need to be put out of the way.' This was attributed to a 'discussion board'.

The Sangh *parivar* has always been ambivalent about Gandhi and felt embarrassed if asked to denounce Godse. The sin is denounced, but the sinner is spared. The BJP's then Vice-President Ram Jethmalani said at Cochin on April 13, 1981 that Godse and Gandhi 'shared the same political philosophy of a united India'.[16] In the first place, Gandhi's and Godse's 'political philosophy' was very different from each other. But even if Jethmalani meant only belief in a united India (and not a shared political philosophy), then surely, millions shared this. Why single out *Godse*? The answer is simple: to belittle the gravity of his crime and, indeed, to cast him in a favourable light.[17] Others are less candid. Nine years earlier, the RSS mouthpiece *Organiser* remembered Godse in these revealing terms: 'It was in support of Nehru's pro-Pakistan stand that Gandhiji went on fast and, in the process, turned *the people's wrath* on himself'.[18] So Godse represented 'the people' and the murder he perpetrated was an expression of 'the people's wrath'. In 1961 Deen Dayal Upadhyaya said: 'With all respect for Gandhiji let us cease to call him Father of the Nation. If we understand the old basis of nationalism, then it will be clear that it is nothing but Hinduism'.[19]

Where the BJP prevaricates, its ally, Shiv Sena's supremo Bal Thackeray, is characteristically blunt and crude. On May 16, 1991, he said in Pune: 'We are proud of Nathuram. He saved the country from a second partition'. He added, 'Nathuram was not a hired assassin. He was genuinely infuriated by Mahatma Gandhi's betrayal of the nation'. The killing of any person 'was an evil act and it should be condemned'. But 'we must find out the reason behind such incidents. The policy of Hindutva alone can save the country from further deterioration'.[20] This was said at an election meeting. Since the BJP was in alliance with the Shiv Sena, four days later the BJP General Secretary Pramod Mahajan was asked at Mumbai to explain his party's stand on this. He 'refused to condemn' the utterances. His party 'does not condemn or support Thackeray's statement. Violence is unjustifiable.'[21] Advani, likewise, called the murder a 'heinous sin' but refused to condemn Thackeray's remarks.[22] No wonder: Thackeray had challenged the BJP to break the alliance if they disapproved of the remarks. *The Times of India* was not impressed. 'Since Mr Thackeray's statement was made *from a BJP election* platform, it is necessary for the BJP to go much further in its rejoinder to the comments.'[23] The paper need not have been surprised at the party's equivocation. Two years earlier, it had editorially noted: 'Mr Advani while holding forth on "Bharat Mata", now goes so far as to deny that Mahatma Gandhi was the Father of the Nation'.[24]

## Savarkar's political career

The truly heroic figure of Gandhi does not draw high praise from BJP and RSS leaders. Savarkar does. What was so heroic about him even if one were to accept his supporters' claims at their face value? Lofty nationalism? A noble vision? Unremitting sacrifice? Courage? Intellectual gifts of a high order? Nobility of character? Not one phase of his chequered career reflects any of these. Even during the early nationalist phase in London, the record is a gravely flawed one. Recently, while inaugurating a park in New Delhi named after

Savarkar and unveiling his statue there, Advani claimed that he was a great freedom fighter and revolutionary who was sent to the Andamans for his revolutionary activities.[25] This is simply not true. Savarkar was sent to Andaman on his conviction for complicity in a brutal and wanton murder. He had narrowly escaped conviction for another murder, which he had instigated. In neither case did he hold the gun. *He never did in any of the cases of murder in which he was involved.* In each, he goaded the assassin, but covered his own tracks skillfully. This is a far cry from other revolutionaries, who were never afraid to wield the gun when needed.

A fair and definitive biography of Savarkar is yet to appear. The standard work in English is Dhananjay Keer's biography which often borders on hagiography. Savarkar died on February 26, 1966 at the age of 83. Before the year was out, Dhanajay Keer published a second edition under a new title *Veer Savarkar.*[26] In his Preface to the second edition Keer wrote, 'the valuable new information and new facts I could get through research and through a plethora of *new material* which was kindly made available to me by *Savarkar himself* and through his kind interviews, were inserted at their proper places in historical sequences'. One wonders whether Savarkar also stipulated that they should be published only after his death. The interval of sixteen years between the two editions is inexplicable on any other assumption. It is noteworthy that most of these additions reflect poorly on Savarkar. For example, Keer leaves out a crucial sentence which points towards Savarkar's complicity in the murder of William Curzon Wylie by Madanlal Dhingra in 1909, as well as, later, in an attempted murder by V.G. Gogate in 1931. Curiously, however, Keer also does not mention in the first edition that Savarkar 'was not a believer in God'. It is unlikely that Keer discovered this after 1950. Clearly, this fact was suppressed for fear of offending Savarkar's orthodox Hindu followers. His suppression of these facts reflects poorly on both the biographer and his subject. Most damagingly, however, Keer suppressed in both editions Savarkar's offer in February 1948 to abjure politics in order to avert prosecution for conspiracy to murder Gandhi. We shall look at all that in some detail below; for the moment, let us trace the evolution of Savarkar's worldview and political career.

Savarkar was born on May 28, 1883 at Bhagur, a village near Nasik in Maharashtra. He was a Chitpavan brahman. When he was ten, he heard of communal riots in the United Provinces and in Mumbai. Keer records:

> the news of the atrocities then perpetrated on the Hindus in the United Provinces and Bombay fired his blood and he resolved to avenge the woes and deaths of his co-religionists. The boy Savarkar led a batch of selected school-mates in a march upon the village mosque. The battalion of these boys showered stones upon it, shattered its windows and tiles and returned victorious. This incident gives the first hint of the heroic mettle Vinayak was made of and the key to his future daring life and leadership.[27]

He had two brothers. Ganesh alias Babarao was the elder brother and Narayan was the younger. While at college he actively participated in a secret society Mitra Mela, which was later renamed Abhinav Bharat. Vinayak went to London to read for the Bar exams there. Like other Indian students of his time, he came into contact with a wide range of political figures, British and Indian. On October 24, 1909 Gandhi presided over a Dasara Sammelan which Savarkar addressed. He said, 'Hindus are the heart of Hindustan. . . . Nevertheless, just as the beauty of the rainbow is not impaired but enhanced by its varied hues, so also Hindustan will appear all the more beautiful across the sky of the future by *assimilating* all that is best in the Muslim, Parsi, Jewish and other civilizations'.[28]

### A tale of two murders

Meanwhile in India, branches of Abhinav Bharat were detected. A few small factories of bombs and secret stores were unearthed in Maharashtra after the arrest of Babarao. He was sentenced to transportation for life on June 8, 1909 on a charge of abetment to waging war against the King. A report compiled by the Intelligence Bureau in Delhi entitled *Terrorism in India 1917–1936* recorded what followed. 'Within a few days his brother, Vinayak Savarkar, made a most seditious speech at the India House in London. This speech was followed within twelve days by the murder of Colonel Sir William Curzon Wylie, Political A.D.C. at the India Office. In December of the same year the District Magistrate of Nasik [M.T. Jackson], who had committed Ganesh Savarkar for trial, was shot dead. Three men were hanged and in a conspiracy case which followed, twenty-seven were sentenced to imprisonment.'[29]

It is necessary to dwell at some length on these two murders because they marked the initiation of Savarkar's 'revolutionary' activity which led to his transportation for life to the Cellular Prison. M.R. Jayakar was a prominent leader of the Hindu Sangathan movement and of the Hindu Mahasabha in the twenties. Vinayak Savarkar presided over it from 1937 to 1942. This is what Jayakar had to say about the trial of Babarao and B.B. Bhopatkar in his memoirs:

> [T]he feeling at the Bar, which I shared fully, was in strong disapproval of the attitude adopted by the accused in both these cases and it was felt that the level of dignity, *courage and integrity* which the cause of Indian freedom had reached during the two previous trials of Tilak and Paranjpe had been *immeasurably lowered by the attitude of the accused in these two later cases.*[30]

In London William Curzon Wylie fell victim to bullets fired by Madanlal Dhingra on the night of July 1, 1909. Along with him fell Dr Cawas Lalkaka who tried to save his life. The murder was committed in the Hall of the Imperial Institute in London at the conclusion of a meeting held to celebrate the annual function of the National Indian Association. Keer's account is particularly noteworthy:

> [Madanlal] was a devoted follower of Savarkar. . . . A few days before the Wylie incident, Dhingra had asked his leader whether the time for martyrdom had really come. Out came the epigrammatic reply from Savarkar, 'If a martyr is

> determined and ready that fact by itself generally implies that the time for martyrdom must have come.'. . . Lord Curzon [former Viceroy of India] was Dhingra's immediate target.[31]

He escaped, fortuitously. Wylie was the next target.

What Keer left unsaid in his book, published while Savarkar was alive, he confided, after his death, to Robert Payne:

> In 1909 he [Savarkar] had shown that he was perfectly capable of ordering a young Indian to murder Sir Curzon Wylie. To his biographer Dhananjay Keer, . . . *he claimed full credit for the murder.* He had given Madanlal Dhingra a nickel-plated revolver, saying curtly, '*Don't show me your face if you fail this time*'. Dhingra had acted like an automation, blindly obedient to him, convinced that he was sacrificing himself on the altar of India's freedom and throughout the trial Savarkar continually encouraged him in the belief that he was a martyr whose name would be remembered for centuries. The London police strongly suspected Savarkar of complicity in the crime, but there was never enough evidence to convict him. He was finally convicted of complicity in the murder of Mr Jackson at the Nasik Conspiracy Trial and sentenced to transportation for life.
>
> The memory of this earlier murder hovered like a ghostly presence over the trial at the Red Fort [the Gandhi murder trial in 1948] never mentioned in court, forgotten except by the oldest members of the audience who crowded the public benches. Savarkar had achieved respectability and his crimes had taken place so long ago that they could be discovered only in the crumbling pages of ancient newspapers. He was responsible for the murders of Sir Curzon Wylie and Mr Jackson, although the weapons had been wielded by others. The prosecution contended that he had engaged in a secret conspiracy with Godse and Apte, and was legally responsible for the murder of Gandhi.[32]

Keer's later disclosure explains Payne's comment:

> Many years passed before the full story of Madanlal Dhingra became known. There was some truth in Gandhi's statement that he [Dhingra] was innocent. He had fallen completely under the domination of Savarkar and scarcely knew what he was doing. Savarkar had been training him for many months, preparing for the day when he would become a martyr to the cause of India. Then, for having failed [to kill Lord Curzon] Dhingra became all the more the creature of Savarkar who continually taunted him for missing a perfect opportunity. On the morning of the assassination of Sir Curzon Wylie, Savarkar gave Dhingra a nickelplated revolver and said 'Don't show me your face if you fail this time'.[33]

Keer however did not quote this crucial statement in the first edition of his biography published in 1950 during Savarkar's lifetime. He did so only in the second edition published in December 1966 after Savarkar's death.[34] A written statement in his defence was found on Dhingra's person at the time of his arrest. It was written by Savarkar.

Suspicion for complicity in Wylie's murder fell instantly on Savarkar. Later in the year, on December 29, 1909, the District Magistrate and Collector of Nasik District, A.M.T. Jackson was shot dead at a theatre. The assassin Anant Kanhere was arrested. Keer holds that Ganpat Savarkar's 'terrific transportation was avenged thus'. Jackson, however, did not try Ganpat Savarkar. He merely committed him to trial by the Sessions Court. There is a particular poignancy about this murder. Jayakar notes:

> Collector Jackson was a reputed Sanskrit scholar and, it was believed, a great admirer of Indians, their language and literature. He was, therefore, it was alleged, posted at Nasik specially to cure the city of its disaffection. Jackson's reputation, as a friendly official, was wide and his literacy

> activities related mostly to writing papers and making speeches about ancient Indian classics.[35]

He was at a theatre to watch the popular Marathi play *Sharada* when Kanhere shot him. Kanhere was a brave man who was anxious to join military service. He was barred from it. A promising career came to an untimely and tragic end by his conviction and sentence to death. Sadly, a far more promising career was arrested and diverted to disastrous course by these events.

### Savarkar's classic

Savarkar worked hard for months at the India Office library doing research for his work *The First Indian War of Independence – 1857.* It was written originally in Marathi in 1908 when Savarkar was about twenty-four years old. Devoted friends studying for the Bar or the Indian Civil Service worked on an English translation. It was published in London in 1909 and was instantly proscribed. The ban was lifted in 1946. The English translation was published in Mumbai in 1947.[36] There are whole pages of *Indian War of Independence* which move the reader even now as they did very many Indians during British rule when they read proscribed copies of the book in clandestine circulation. It is a veritable classic.

Savarkar's subsequent career should not blind one to that outstanding achievement, still less to the message which Savarkar sought then to convey to fellow Indians, Hindus and Muslims alike. It was history written with a noble purpose. The careful reader, however, cannot but be disturbed by portions of the book which reflect a warped notion of India's past and, worse, the spirit of revenge and a passion for violence. These explain why Savarkar adopted the course he did later.[37] But he might not have were it not for his involvement in the murders of Wyllie and Jackson.

Arrested along with Jackson's assailant Anant Kanhere were other conspirators. Letters from Savarkar were found in their possession and the Browning pistol which Kanhere had used was traced to him. The government of the huge Presidency of Bombay thereupon issued a telegraphic warrant for Savarkar's arrest under the Fugitive Offenders Act, 1881. He was in Paris then but decided to give himself up to the police. He was arrested at the Victoria Station in London on March 13, 1910. The charges were waging war or abetting the waging of war against His Majesty the King Emperor of India, conspiring to deprive the King of the sovereignty of British India or a part of it, procuring and distributing arms and abetting the murder of Jackson, procuring and distributing arms in London and waging war from London, and delivering seditious speeches in India from January to March, 1906 and in London from 1908 to 1909.

Savarkar's escape through a port-hole of *S.S. Morea* on July 8, 1910, when it anchored at Marseilles, and his immediate capture on French soil lent an aura of romance to his fame as a revolutionary. He was brought to Mumbai on July 22, 1910 and was tried by a Special Tribunal comprising the Chief Justice of Bombay High Court, Sir Basil Scott, Justice Sir N.G. Chandavarkar and Justice Sir John Heaton. A formidable defence team was lead by Joseph Baptista. The tribunal sat on three trials from September 15, 1910 onwards. The first involved thirty-eight accused, including Savarkar. The second involved him and a co-accused in the first case, Gopalrao Patankar. In the last, Savarkar was the sole accused. Savarkar was alleged to have sent twenty Browning pistols to his associates in India.[38]

The hearings lasted for sixty-nine days. On December 24, 1910, Savarkar was sentenced to transportation for life and forfeiture of all his property, in the first case. The second trial for abetment of Jackson's murder opened on January 23, 1911. A week later, he was sentenced to *another* term of transportation for life-fifty years in the Andamans. The Government rejected a very reasonable plea of Savarkar that the two sentences run concurrently as is normally the case.[39]

We have a much more objective account of the Nasik Conspiracy case from the devoted historian of the Bombay High Court, P.B. Vachha.[40] Like Jayakar, Vachha pays rich tributes to Jackson. 'He was sympathetic towards Indian aspirations.' He adds: 'From the evidence, it was clear that Savarkar [with his two brothers] was the brain, leader, and moving spirit of the conspiracy'.

### Apology upon apology

Savarkar was brought to Port Blair, capital of the Andamans on July 4, 1911. But before the year ended, he submitted 'a petition for clemency'. Its text is not available. But he refers to it in yet another petition dated November 14, 1913.[41] The 1913 petition addressed the Home Member of the Governor-General's Executive Council, Reginald Craddock, as 'your honour', reminded him of 'the petition for clemency that I had sent in 1911', and promised to

> serve the Government in any capacity they like, for as my conversion is conscientious, so I hope my future conduct would be. By keeping me in jail nothing can be got in comparison to what would be otherwise. The Mighty alone can afford to be merciful and therefore where else can the prodigal son return but to the parental doors of the Government.

No apology, no plea for clemency can be more abject and demeaning than this. It by itself suffices to render Savarkar unworthy of admiration or respect. All the more so when it is viewed as part of *a pattern of conduct in which he invariably uses another person to fire a gun and enthusiastically provides any undertaking, any apology to escape the consequences of his misdeed.* These two petitions were not known to any one in India. They were concealed even from his brother Narayan.

Two other such undertakings bear recalling here. Savarkar was brought back from the Andamans and lodged in the Ratnagiri Jail and moved thereafter to the Yeravada Jail in Pune. What Keer euphemistically describes as 'helpful winds' blowing in Savarkar's direction were the result of his and his family's frantic efforts to secure release on any terms. Keer records:

> Sir George Lloyd, the Governor of Bombay, came with his Councillors to interview Savarkar. . . . The conditions of release were prepared in the light of the discussions held between Savarkar and H.E. the Governor and his

> Councillors. After substituting a few words, Savarkar accepted the conditions, signed the terms and was released conditionally on January 6, 1924, from the Yeravada Jail. The terms read:
> 1. that Savarkar shall reside in the Ratnagiri District and shall not go beyond the limits of that District without the permission of Government or in case of emergency of the District Magistrate.
> 2. that he will not engage publicly or privately in any manner of political activities without the consent of Government for a period of five years such restrictions being renewable at the discretion of Government at the expiry of the said term.[42]

Keer omits to mention another document, just as abject as this, written by Savarkar. In a seminal article, Krishnan Dubey and Venkitesh Ramakrishnan write:

> Savarkar accepted these conditions without any compunction. But this was not all. Seeing his spirit broken and will power completely shattered, the Government suggested that he should state that his trial was fair and the sentence awarded was just. At the same time, it told him this was 'in no way made a condition of his release'. Yet, he went ahead and made this statement, 'I hereby acknowledge that I had a fair trial and just sentence. I heartily abhor methods of violence resorted to in days gone by, and I feel myself duty bound to uphold Law and the constitution to the best of my powers and am willing to make the Reform a success insofar as I may be allowed to do so in future.'
>
> The reference to the Reform here is to the Montagu-Chelmsford proposals of 1918 which fell woefully short of Indian expectations. . . . Savarkar went out of his way to offer his mite to make them a success. Soon after his release, Dr K.B. Hedgewar, the founder of the Rashtriya Swayamsewak Sangh (RSS), came to meet Savarkar in Ratnagiri, he is said to have obtained Savarkar's

wholehearted support to the founding of the RSS, which was inaugurated on Vijayadasami day, 1925.

The story of Savarkar's surrender to British imperialism does not end here. In February 1925, serious communal trouble broke out in Kohat town of the North-West Frontier Province (NWFP). Jivan Das of Kohat had written a booklet, *Rangila Rasool,* portraying Prophet Mohammed in bad light. This caused communal riots in Kohat, in other towns in the NWFP and in the western parts of the then Punjab. As rumours spread throughout the country, Savarkar felt so agitated he wrote an article in the *Mahratta* of Pune on March 1, 1925.

The Government did not take to this kindly. He was warned that 'any future writings of a similar character will be regarded by Government a sufficient justification for reconsidering the question of his release'. Post-haste, despite his having very strong views on the Kohat incidents, Savarkar sent a longish explanation at the end of which he thanked the Government for having given him an opportunity to explain himself and hoped that in future too they would be pleased to be as kindly disposed towards him. In this letter, dated April 6, he made it clear he would have no truck with the idea of Swaraj: '*The only place where the word Swaraj occurs is at the end of the third paragraph and there it is obvious that a reference is not at all to show or indicate what I or other people think of Swaraj but in what exaggerated terms Mr Gandhi thinks of Khilafat.*'

The Government was not mollified even by this. It told him curtly on May 6, 1925 it considered his explanation far from satisfactory. '. . . it should have been obvious to you that an article of the nature which you published in the issue of *Mahratta* of the 1st March, 1925 was bound to inflame the feelings and increase the tensions between Hindus and Muhammadans and was contrary to your undertaking not to engage in any manner in political activities without the consent of Government.'

This letter was received by Savarkar on May 8

> through the District Magistrate. It so unnerved him that the very next day he wrote back to D. O'Flynn, Acting Deputy Secretary to the Government of Bombay, Home Department, thus, '. . . I most humbly beg to request in as much as this order came to my hand on the 8$^{th}$ of May, all my writings and speeches prior to that date should not be subjected to that interpretation as they were guided by the first or direct interpretation I naturally put on the meaning of terms of my conditions of release.'
>
> Savarkar took fright that the Government might resort to some severe action against him for some of writings and speeches made between March and May 8. One warning from the Government, and his concern for the so-called welfare of Hindus had disappeared into thin air.[43]

So submissive, even obsequious, was he that on some occasions Savarkar dictated the summary of his important speeches to the District Magistrate as a precaution. Keer records: 'The mere word "Swaraj" or "Raj" in his article or speech was highly resented by the British government and many a time he was threatened with dire consequences'.[44] Little did Keer reckon when he wrote this that someday a scholar would trace Savarkar's letter of April 6, 1925 and show that Savarkar virtually apologized for using the word 'Swaraj'!

## The unseen hands of the zealot

The five-year term was extended in 1929 by two years and again in 1931, 1933 and 1935. The Government of India Act, 1935, which came into force on April 1, 1937, conferred autonomy on the Provinces. It was widely expected that after the general elections to the Provincial Assemblies under the Act, a popular Congress ministry would assume office in Bombay, as in other Provinces. Negotiations were under way between the Congress and the British. Meanwhile, an interim Ministry took office in Bombay comprising Khan Bahadur Dhanjishaw Cooper with the support of the Hindu Mahasabhaite Jamnadas M. Mehta. Savarkar was released by them on May 10, 1937.

But, not before incurring suspicion for instigating yet

another attempted murder. The Intelligence Bureau's Report has this to narrate:

> Poona was also the scene of one of the most serious terrorist crimes which have been perpetrated in Bombay Presidency. Sir Ernest Hotson, the acting Governor, was making an informal visit to the Ferguson College, Poona, on July 22nd, 1931, when a student, Vasudev Balavant Gogate, suddenly took out a revolver and fired two shots at him. The first bullet was deflected by the stud of a notebook in His Excellency's pocket and the second went wide. Sir Ernest was not hurt and immediately tackled and secured his assailant with the help of his ADC who found another revolver on Gogate. The ensuing behaviour of the other students was far from satisfactory, cries of 'Shame' were made when Gogate was removed by the police, and had obtained the revolvers and ammunition from Hyderabad, Deccan. He gave his motive as a personal hatred of Sir Ernest Hotson in being appointed to officiate as Governor in preference to an Indian. Gogate was sentenced to eight years' rigorous imprisonment.[45]

Robert Payne's investigations into Gandhi's murder, on January 30, 1948, yielded this nugget of information:

> On the night of January 26, Nathuram Godse, Apte and Karkare held a secret meeting in the freight yard of the Thana railroad station in the outskirts of Bombay. They talked in whispers. Godse said he was afraid Pahwa would talk to the police and there was only a little time left. In his view the original plan involving nine or ten conspirators was a mistake, it would be better if one man did the deed, and he had long ago come to the conclusion that he was the one who should do it. He spoke about Madanlal Dhingra *and Vasudev Rao Gogate, both of whom were commanded by Savarkar to commit murder.* Madanlal Dhingra had shot Sir Curzon Wylie in London. Vasudev Rao Gogate had shot at

> the Governor of Bombay in 1931. The Governor had not been killed, because he was wearing a bulletproof vest, but Gogate's name had been held in high honour by the Hindu Mahasabha ever since.[46]

In the 1966 edition of his book, Keer acknowledged that 'Gogate was a staunch Savarkarite and had met Savarkar in Ratnagiri some days before he shot the hot-headed Hotson.'[47] Again, this is something Keer suppressed in the first edition.

Now read what K.M. Munshi, Home Minister of Bombay Presidency (1937–39), a Congressman with pronounced sympathies for the Hindu Mahasabha and the RSS, had to say of Gogate:

> Another instance in which the Governor had unwillingly to accept my advice related to the release of V.B. Gogate, a young college student and a *disciple of Vinayak Damodar Savarkar.*
>
> He was undergoing life sentence for having made an attempt to assassinate a former Home Member of the Government of Bombay, Sir Ernest Hotson, who at the time was officiating as the Governor, when he was on a visit to a college in Poona. Lord Brabourne would not accept my advice. He said, 'Attempts at assassinating a Governor are a serious matter.'
>
> I did not press the issue on that occasion. However, I immediately wrote a letter to Sir Ernest Hotson, who happened to be my friend, asking him to help me in the matter by agreeing to release Gogte, the gesture, I pointed out, would help the new Ministry. A few days later, Lord Brabourne called me. He was annoyed that I should have written to Hotson directly about Gogte's matter. He had received a communication from the Viceroy that Hotson had no objection to his accepting my advice.[48]

It is unlikely that Munshi would have exerted himself thus for a Muslim communalist and terrorist.

It is well known and obvious from their work that Larry Collins and Dominique Lapierre had access to police and intelligence reports. They wrote extensively about Savarkar's involvements, particularly in Gandhi's murder. They claimed that he 'had subsequently [after his release] organized the assassination of the Governor of the Punjab' – on this, to be fair, no corroborative material whatever is available – 'and an unsuccessful attempt on the life of the governor of Bombay'. Thus, all three – Payne, Collins and Lapierre – agree on Savarkar's complicity in the Gogate affair. Munshi noted that he was a follower of Savarkar. Collins and Lapierre remarked 'The Andaman Islands, however, had taught Savarkar a lesson. He concealed his connections with the killers so carefully that the police were never able to build a case against him.'[49] They described him as 'the zealot whose unseen hands had controlled the flow of at least three political assassinations' – those of Curzon Wilie, Jackson and Gandhi. Savarkar was convicted only in the Jackson case. Material has come to light, especially after his death, which strengthens suspicion of his complicity held even while he was alive.

In subsequent chapters we offer a detailed account of Savarkar's behaviour in the Andamans based on his own writings (chapter 3), an analysis of his essay *Hindutva* (1923), its impact on the RSS and influence on the BJP, and his role in Indian politics (chapter 4). His widely suspected involvement in Gandhi's murder is discussed in chapter 5 in detail. For the moment, let us note that a Commission of Inquiry headed by a former Judge of the Supreme Court, Justice J.L. Kapur, held the belief to be well founded. The Commission observed, after a recital of damning evidence: 'All these facts taken together were destructive of any theory other than the conspiracy to murder by Savarkar and his group.'[50]

In the nearly forty years between 1913 and 1950, then, Savarkar did not change. He would prostrate himself before the Government to escape the consequences of his actions. The pattern in these actions too was constant – use another to pull the trigger at one whom Savarkar had picked to be killed. He would lie at the drop of a hat. At the trial he dishonestly denied a fact known to all who knew him and Nathuram Godse – their closeness. Even Keer acknowledged this.[51] So did Nathuram's brother Gopal. The Kapur Report confirms that.

### The two-nation theory

Savarkar was the first to propound the two-nation theory. He propounded it first in *Hindutva* in 1923 and next in his Presidential Address to the Hindu Mahasabha on December 30, 1937: 'There are two nations in the main: The Hindu and the Moslems in India.' An year later, in 1938, he said: 'the Hindus are the nation in India – in Hindusthan, and the Moslem minority a community'.[52]

R.C. Majumdar, a historian with pronounced pro-Sangh *parivar* sympathies, acknowledged that there was 'one important factor which was responsible to a very large extent for the emergence of the idea of partition of India on communal lines. This was the Hindu Mahasabha . . .' Savarkar was, to him, 'the great revolutionary leader.'[53] He added that 'the Muslim League took serious notice of the frank [sic] speeches of Savarkar.' Jinnah propounded *his* two-nation theory in 1939. It divided the country he once loved, harmed the community he led, and blighted the future of the State he founded. Pakistan broke up in 1971, exposing the falsity of the theory. Thirty years later it is still in the grip of sectarian religious strife. Jinnah himself discarded his theory in 1947. The two-nation theory is intrinsically poisonous, but it becomes all the more pernicious when it proceeds to assert that not only are the two communities *different,* but that one is *inferior* to the other. That was Savarkar's belief throughout his life.

Hatred came naturally to him. In 1925, Jayakar invited him to a public meeting at the Vedanta Ashram:

> Some eminent speakers participated. Among them, Savarkar the Hindu Sabha leader made an extraordinary speech, the main theme of which was that, until we are a free nation, we must not think of practicing soft virtue like humility, self-surrender or forgiveness. On the Contrary, we must, during our subjection, develop sturdy habits of hatred, retaliation, vindictiveness and such other features. In other

> words, we must postpone, until we are free, the virtues inculcated by our religion. Though this speech was delivered in attractive language, there was commotion in the audience. Savarkar strengthened his argument by misconceiving Tilak's observation that Indians must postpone the delights, the ease and dignity of scholarship and research until India was free. A few speakers supported Savarkar's view, though a large majority differed and the danger appeared to be that a meeting called chiefly to popularize the lofty teachings of Shri Ramakrishna was likely to be misused for the propagation, in the name of patriotism, of views bordering on spiteful retaliation, vengeful hatred, vindictive punishment and the like.[54]

In a detailed critique of Hindutva, Dr B.R. Ambedkar shows his definition of a Hindu –which forms the basis of Hindutva – 'has been framed with great care and caution'. A Hindu is one who regards India as *both* his Fatherland (Pithrubhoomi) as well as his Holyland (Punyabhoomi). 'It is designed to serve two purposes which Mr Savarkar has in view. First, to exclude from it Muslims, Christians, Parsis and Jews by prescribing the recognition of India as Holy Land as a qualification of being a Hindu. Secondly, to include Buddhists, Jains, Sikhs, etc., by not insisting upon belief in the sanctity of the Vedas as an element in the qualifications.'[55]

It is a man with this divisive credo whom the BJP lauds as a national hero. Speaking at a function to launch a book on Bhagat Singh at New Delhi on February 25, 2000, Vajpayee went out of his way to drag in Savarkar's name. He 'maintained that the contribution of RSS theoretician Veer Savarkar and others was no less than that of Shaheed Bhagat Singh and his compatriots.'[56] No two persons could have been more different than Bhagat Singh and Savarkar. Bhagat Singh wielded the gun himself twice, knowing, on the second occasion, in the Central Assembly, on April 8, 1929, that escape was impossible. Savarkar repeatedly used others to kill the one he hated. Bhagat Singh was a man of noble disposition. Savarkar wallowed in hate. Bhagat Singh was an Indian nationalist. He distanced himself from Lala Lajpat Rai, when his mentor turned communal. Savarkar was a Hindu nationalist who spread communal hate. Bhagat Singh was generous to a fault. Savarkar was mean even to those close to him. In prison Bhagat Singh realized the futility of violence and wrote against its use. Savarkar's mindset protected him from such realization. Bhagat Singh refused to plead for mercy even when he faced the gallows – in fact, he pleaded that he and his comrades be shot dead like prisoners of war rather than hung, since they were guilty of waging war against the British empire. He wrote a sharp letter to his father asking not to write in his defense to the Tribunal trying him. Savarkar's is a remarkably consistent record of sheer cowardice.[57] Every terrorist of old wielded the gun himself, led a life of self-denial, had a noble vision of India, was prepared to lay down his life for his country. The prospect of death did not deter him. In all this, Savarkar presents a contrast in disgrace. He would cringe and prostrate at the first opportunity when forced with imprisonment. He was a merchant of hate. He was heavily subsidized by well-known financiers, as the archives reveal.

### The Gandhi murder

One is constrained to ask – *is there any revolutionary in the history of any country whose record is as scarred as Savarkar's?* What drives the BJP to acclaim him as a hero is his authorship of Hindutva, the credo of communal hate. For this, all his other sins are overlooked. There is an aspect to the Gandhi murder case which has been commonly overlooked. Since the conspiracy originated in the erstwhile Bombay Province, it is the Bombay Police which conducted the investigation into its ramifications. But the Delhi Police came in because the dastardly murder was perpetrated in Delhi. There was perfect rapport between Morarji Desai, Home Minister of Bombay, and Vallabhbhai Patel, the Union Home Minister. In any case, there is no charge sheet in a case such as this unless Patel approved of it. His devotion to Gandhi was total. He was, besides, an outstandingly able criminal lawyer in his time. *Savarkar could not have been cited as one of the accused unless Patel had approved of it.* The record reflects creditably on Patel and as poorly on his ill-chosen cabinet colleague, Shyama Prasad Mookerjee, himself a former President of the Mahasabha, supporter of Savarkar, and subsequently founder of the Jan Sangh.

Mookerjee rushed to write to Patel on May 4, 1948,

> I wrote to you (and also spoke to Shankar) about the definition of persons connected with the Mahasabha. Those who are suspected of complicity in the outrage on Gandhiji will no doubt be put up for trial. I understand Savarkar's name is being mentioned in this connection. I do not know what evidence has been found against him. I have not the least doubt that you will satisfy yourself that nothing is done which may give rise to the suggestion later on that was prosecuted on account of his political convictions. I hope the records will be placed before you before any decision is taken. His sacrifices and suffering in the past have been considerable and unless there is some positive proof against him, he should not, at this age, be subjected to charge of conspiracy to commit murder. I leave the matter to your decision.[58]

Patel replied thus on May 6, 1948:

> As regards Savarkar, the Advocate-General of Bombay, who is in charge of the case, and other legal advisers and investigating officers met me at conference in Delhi before I came here. I told them, quite clearly, that the question of inclusion of Savarkar must be approached *purely from a legal and judicial standpoint* and political considerations should not be imported into the matter. My instructions were quite definite and beyond doubt and I am sure they will be acted upon. I have also told them that, if they come to the view that Savarkar should be included, *the papers should be placed before me before action is taken.* This is, of course, in so far as the question of guilt is concerned from the point of view of *law* and justice. *Morally*, it is possible that one's conviction may be the other way about.[59]

What else did Patel mean by that except that even if Savarkar's guilt not be established before the court, 'morally' it was possible to hold him guilty of the crime? The charge sheet against the accused, including Savarkar, was filed in Court on May 27, 1948 when the trial commenced. But, earlier, on May 15, a notification in the Gazette of India Extraordinary published the names of nine accused persons. Savarkar was the eighth accused.[60]

To continue with Patel's reply to Mookerjee:

> I quite agree with you that the Hindu Mahasabha, as an organization, was not concerned in the conspiracy that led to Gandhi's murder, but at the same time, we cannot shut our eyes to the fact that an appreciable number of the members of the Mahasabha gloated over the tragedy and distributed sweets. On this matter, reliable reports have come to us from all parts of the country. Further, militant communalism, which was preached until only a few months ago by many spokesmen of the Mahasabha, including men like Mahant Digbijoy Nath, Prof. Ram Singh and Deshpande, could not but be regarded as a danger to public security. *The same would apply to the RSS* with the additional danger inherent in an organization run in secret on military or semi-military lines.[61]

No one has alleged, to this day, that the RSS, 'as an organization' was privy to Gandhi's murder. That would imply direction at its highest level, by its chief or executive. What has been alleged – and was for long frantically denied – was that Godse *was a member of the RSS.* The cover was finally blown away by Gopal Godse at a press conference, in Pune on June 5, 1991, when he said that Nathuram was a volunteer of the RSS, but the RSS was not involved in the assassination.[62]

Mookerjee wrote to Patel again on July 17, 1948 on 'our policy towards RSS and Hindu Mahasabha', pleading that neither was involved as an organization ('as such'). He pleaded for 'Hindu consolidation' inspite of 'political differences between party and party. . . . Hindus holding strong views on the need for saving India from passing under Muslim rule or other foreign rule should not be dubbed as fascist or conspirators.' An entire section was devoted on 'our attitude towards Muslims' to allege that they were disloyal to India.[63]

Patel replied the very next day on July 18:

> As regards *the RSS* and *the Hindu Mahasabha*, the case relating to Gandhiji's murder is *sub judice* and I should not like to say anything about the participation of the two organizations, but our reports do confirm that, *as a result of the activities of these two bodies, particularly the former, an atmosphere was created in the country in which such a ghastly tragedy became possible.* There is no doubt in my mind that *the extreme section of the Hindu Mahasabha was involved in this conspiracy.* The activities of the RSS constituted a clear threat to the existence of Government and the State. Our reports show that those activities, despite the ban, have not died down. Indeed, as time has marched on, the RSS circles are becoming more defiant and are indulging in their subversive activities in an increasing measure.[64]

Which was this 'extreme section of the Hindu Mahasabha involved in this conspiracy?' Patel did not identify it explicitly. But he knew quite well who its leader was. It is unlikely that Mookerjee understood this to refer to Godse *alone, not* Savarkar. Indeed, in a letter to Prime Minister Jawaharlal Nehru on February 27, 1948, Patel had told all:

> *I have kept myself almost in daily touch with the progress of the investigation regarding Bapu's assassination case.* I devote a large part of my evening to discussing with Sanjevi the day's progress and giving instructions to him on any points that arise. All the main accused have given long and detailed statements of their activities. In one case, the statement extends to ninety typed pages. From their statements, it is quite clear that no part of the conspiracy took place in Delhi.

> The centers of activity were Poona, Bombay, Ahmedabad and Gwalior. Delhi was, of course, the terminating point of their activity, but by no means its centre; nor do they seem to have spent more than a day or two at a time, and that too only twice between 19 and 30 January. It also clearly emerges from these statements that the RSS was not involved in it at all. It was a fanatical wing of the Hindu Mahasabha directly under Savarkar that (hatched) the conspiracy and saw it through. . . . Of course, his assassination was welcomed by those of the RSS and the Mahasabha who were strongly opposed to his way of thinking and to his policy. But beyond this, I do not think it is possible, on the evidence which has come before us, to implicate any other members of the RSS or the Hindu Mahasabha.[65]

The question brooks no evasion. Why do the BJP and the RSS ignore the mass of material on Savarkar's role in Gandhi's murder and laud him as a hero? Would they have been as quiescent if the assassin had not been the author of Hindutva? Contrast this with their hyperactivity when the Jan Sangh's President Deen Dayal Upadhyaya was found dead on February 11, 1968. He had left Lucknow for Patna the previous evening by Sealdah Express. His dead body was found lying near a traction pole 748 feet from the end of the platform of Mughalsarai station on which the train had halted at about 2.10 a.m. that day. The CBI said that the murder was committed by common thieves for small gain and was executed on the spur of the moment. The Jan Sangh attacked the CBI and set up a Committee, headed by Nana Deshmukh, to collect evidence. He filed his statement of the case and figured as one of the 51 witnesses examined by the Jan Sangh before a Commission of Inquiry. The CBI examined 23 witnesses. The Commission comprised Justice Y.V. Chandrachud of the Bombay High Court who became Chief Justice of India. His Report is a thorough exposure of the tactics to which the Sangh *parivar* readily stoops.[66] The Sessions Judge Varanasi had on June 9, 1969 acquitted both the accused, two young men, Bharat Lal Dom and Ram Awadh, of the charge of murder. Bharat Lal was convicted of theft of Upadhya's belongings and sentenced him to a term of four years. The Commission of Inquiry was set up on October 23, 1969.

The Jan Sangh cast its net wide with a malevolence that defies belief. It alleged that 'Upadhyaya was murdered for political reasons' and accused 'certain Muslim organizations' as well as 'some Communists' of complicity in the crime. They were alleged to have taken 'the help' of one Major S.M. Sharma. He was the son-in-law of one V.N. Sharma 'who in turn is said to be closely connected with Dr. Abdul Jalil Faridi, the President of the Majlis Mushawarat.' A host of others were dragged in. The CBI was alleged to have 'manipulated' the discovery of Upadhyaya's articles and 'concocted evidence.'[67]

Justice Chandrachud's Report, dated October 20, 1970, did more than find these charges to be totally groundless: 'I can say with a certain amount of confidence that nothing that has come before me can support the accusation that there was any politics in Shri Upadhyaya's murder.' It was the rash and 'extempore handiwork of mere thieves'. That however was not all. A diary written by Ramacharya Pandey, a Jan Sangh member and editor of a weekly, was found to be a total fabrication 'for the purpose of producing it as evidence.' Nana Deshmukh himself was disbelieved on an important point:

> I cannot accept Shri Nanaji Deshmukh's statement that he had told Ramacharya on the 11th morning on phone that he should collect the relevant information. Nanaji was then in Bombay and knew nothing about the murder. In fact, there is a good basis for doubting that Ramacharya at all telephoned Nanaji from Lucknow on the 11th morning. Om Prakash Chatwal of the Lucknow Telephone Exchange, who was examined before me by the CBI, has stated that no trunk call was made from telephone number 23509 (Lucknow) to Bombay on the 11th February 1968. 23509 is the telephone number of the Jan Sangh Karyalaya, Lucknow, where Ramacharya says he received the information about Shri Upadhyaya's death.[68]

The Sangh *parivar* manages somehow to live down such behaviour. But how does a figure like Savarkar inspire people to raise statues in his memory and name roads after him? Contrast this with the treatment meted out to those nationalists who were Muslims and who sacrificed no less than their Hindu comrades for their participation in the freedom movement. The historian Prof. Mushirul Hasan's credentials as a scholar and a committed secularist cannot be challenged. His analysis of this tendency bears quotation *in extensor*:

> When the Indian State grudgingly commemorates their memory to advertise its secular credentials, it does so with much fanfare as an act of goodwill to the Muslims, a concession to their sentiments. Organizers are carefully picked from the 'Muslim' intelligentsia and the chosen venue of conferences and symposia are, predictably, the University at Aligarh, the Jamia Millia Islamia and the Khuda Bakhsh Library in Patna.
>
> It is equally extraordinary how an inappropriate expression – Nationalist Muslims – has gained such wide currency and is bandied about to detail the activities of people like Ansari and Azad. Its inappropriateness lies in *the majoritarian view of Indian nationalism* which assumes the presence of nationalistic and patriotic sentiments in the 'majority' community alone. If 'others' shared the same feelings, it is seen as an exception rather than a rule. Thus Ajmal Khan, Ansari and Azad – all 'Nationalist Muslims' – are set apart from their co-religionists. They are treated as exceptional men, uncommon and unique to a community which was structured to favour pan-Islamism and repudiate nationalism.
>
> If Ajmal, Ansari and Azad were 'Nationalist Muslims' because of their loyalty to a particular strand of nationalism, one must surely, by the same logic, designate Gandhi, Nehru and Patel as 'Nationalist Hindus'. Again, if religion is the sole criterion for categorizing an individual or a group, how do we, then, describe a kisan or a trade

> union leader? Was Muzaffar Ahmad a 'Nationalist Muslim' and P.C. Joshi a 'Nationalist Hindu'? It is not enough to search for answers but to provide a corrective to a highly distorted image of India's recent past.
>
> Identities, religious or otherwise, are created through a dialectical process. Often, they are also superimposed in order to lend credence to a stereotyped image of a community. In consequence, the actions of the 'Nationalist Muslims', which should ideally be part of the nationalist discourse, an aspect of the collective memory of a nation, are inextricably intertwined with Muslim alone.[69]

By this impeccable logic, Savarkar should be regarded as a Hindu Nationalist for his espousal of Hindutva from 1923, if not earlier, till his death forty years later, in 1966. That he is nonetheless lauded as an Indian nationalist is one more proof of Nehru's wise warning on January 5, 1961. The communalism of the minority becomes obvious, 'But the communalism of a majority communalism is apt to be taken for nationalism.'[70]

Nehru said this as a reproach to Hindu communalists masquerading as Indian nationalists. Savarkar proved him right in his own perverse manner. Addressing a students' gathering at Kanpur, Savarkar said,

> What is called Nationalism can be defined as in fact the National communalism of the majority community which has been ruling and still aspires to rule this country. Thus, in Hindusthan it is the Hindus, professing Hindu religion and being in overwhelming majority, that constitute the National community and create and formulate the Nationalism of the Nation. It is so in every country of the world. . . . The minorities, while maintaining their separate religions and civilizations cooperate with the majority communities and merge themselves in the common life and administration of these countries.[71]

No wonder the Sangh *parivar* hates Nehru's memory. But it

retains a soft cover for Morarji Desai. It would therefore be fitting to remind them of Desai's carefully-worded judgment on Savarkar in the Bombay Legislative Council on April 3, 1948, when R.N. Mandlik referred to 'the past services of the Savarkar brothers'. Morarji Desai's reply was devastatingly brief: 'May I say, Sir, that the past services are more than offset by the present disservice?'[72]

# 2 SAVARKAR'S NATIONALISM

> IT IS NOT easy for an Indian to write about the Rebellion of 1857, of its blood and tears, its sufferings, heroism and humiliation. Until India regains her freedom the writing will never be free from emotional overtones. '1857' strikes a flint on his heart and sparks fly. Our people do not speak of the events – it is not safe to speak of them – but they hang like stalactites in the caves of our memory. A missionary once asked a group of boys to write an essay on the Mutiny. 'Every youth sent in a sheet of blank paper. It was a silent, unanimous, unapologetic refusal to perform the task.' We have preferred to keep our thoughts to ourselves. With an obstinate silence we have rejected and passed by the spate of literature on the Mutiny that has come from British writers. It, however, continues to stalk through our memory – an unavenged and unappeased ghost.
>
> No English writer on the other hand has succeeded in placing the Mutiny in its proper historical perspective. The British apologist has the advantage of ample material from which to elaborate his arguments. The Indians lost the war, and the records of their side perished with their fighters. No effort has been spared by British writers to besmirch the memory of the martyred heroes of Indian freedom.[1]

These words are from a book on the Revolt of 1857 by Asoka Mehta. For a number of reasons, 1857 must be considered a watershed event in the history of India. One of these is that while 1857 itself widened the chasm between Indians and Europeans, its aftermath created a divide between Hindus and Muslims. Asoka Mehta's analysis is brilliant:

> When the rebellion began Hindus and Muslims participated in it in large numbers. It was not a rebellion of one community. But the Mussalmans, for historical and ideological reasons, were more violently anti-British than the Hindus. To many of them, inspired by the philosophy of Shah Waliulla, India under British rule was *Dar-ul-Harb,* and a jehad against the alien ruler was not only a national necessity but a religious duty. The British, therefore, feared the fiery and excitable Muslim more than the proverbially mild Hindu.
>
> The hand of repression fell heavily on the Muslims – they were as it were tattooed with terror. Many of their leading men – such as the Nawabs of Jhajjar, Ballabgarh, Faruknagar and Farukabad – were hanged or exiled. . . . Muslim property was widely confiscated. After the re-occupation of Delhi, Hindus were allowed to return within a few months, but the Mohammedan population was altogether excluded and the attachment on their houses was lifted only in 1859. In the Delhi Division every Muslim was mulcted of a quarter of his real property while the fine levied on the Hindus was just ten per cent.
>
> The wrath of the rulers was mainly directed against the Muslims. 'Show these rascally Mussulmans,' wrote Capt. Roberts (the future field-Marshal Lord Roberts) 'that with God's help, Englishmen will still be masters of India.' The suffering of the Muslims were great, innocent and guilty alike perished in the flaming vengeance of the victors. The family of even a staunch loyalist like Syed Ahmed Khan paid a heavy toll in hardship and death. The terror and dismay of the time are caught in the letters of Ghalib, '*Shaher sahra ho gaya*' ('The city has become a howling wilderness'). Urdubazar is gone, what then of Urdu? Delhi is no more a

> city, it is a camp – the fort, the town, the bazars, and the canals, all are gone! . . .
>
> The Muslims not only braved more and suffered more in the Mutiny, but they refused to accept defeat and remained unreconciled for a long time. They kept up resistance in different forms . . . . *They rejected English education and thereby steadily lost ground in professions and in the Government services. While the Hindus were absorbing western ideas and adjusting themselves to the new circumstances, the Muslims remained aloof, estranged, wrapped up in their traditional beliefs. The Muslim renaissance that had been growing in Delhi wilted with the Mutiny.* . . . Calcutta, the centre of the Hindu renaissance, on the other hand, had escaped the horrors of the Mutiny and emerged unscathed not only in body but in spirit.
>
> A cleavage thus grew up between the two communities that has developed a veritable schism in the soul of India. *The communal bickerings and disputes that disfigure and poison our civic life are an unhappy legacy of post-Mutiny developments.*[2]

## Savarkar and 1857

As is well-known, Savarkar had also written a book on the Revolt of 1857: *The First Indian War of Independence – 1857.* Of Savarkar's book, Asoka Mehta wrote:

> Few Indians have yet ventured to write on the Mutiny. Vinayak Savarkar is an exception. He carried the torch of research through the dungeons of musty records and produced a valuable book. But it bears the stamp of immaturity, it surges with the passion, poetry and patriotism of youth. Lines, circles, loops of passionate outbursts and historical analyses assemble and unwind themselves in it. It is more of a manifesto than a sober history. The Mutiny awaits its immortal historians.

The criticism is valid, but it is no reason for underestimating the very high quality of Sarvarkar's work as a manifesto. Savarkar wrote history with a purpose. The history, as it turned out, was flawed. The purpose, however, was noble: to unite Hindus and Muslims in the struggle for freedom from British rule and for the establishment, thereafter, of a United States of India in which all would be equal citizens.

Savarkar's subsequent rejection of this ideal has prompted three different kinds of reactions. One is to laud Savarkar's earlier ideal uncritically, as Madhu Limaye did. He argued that India should remember only the early Savarkar.[3] This is an unhistorical view. The incompetence in scholarship is reflected in Limaye nominating 1937 as the turning point in Savarkar's career, ignoring *Hindutva* of 1923, and overlooking some disturbing aspects of *Indian War of Independence* itself. The second approach is to belittle the book because of Savarkar's later politics, which, again, is unhistorical, besides being incompetent scholarship. The third is to treat it as a serious work of history and praise or criticize it as such. This approach is correct, since it entails accepting the work at its face value, accepting Savarkar's word, and discerning accurately, both the nobility of his vision *and the seeds of what blighted it in the years to come*, namely, *a communal misreading of history*. He was prepared to *forgive* the imagined wrongs of the past committed by Muslims which he had hitherto nurtured in his mind. But he had not *forgotten* them, nor shed his misinterpretation. The diversion to a different course was less radical when this flaw is borne in mind. More disturbing than this was his exposure of the dark recesses of his mind. What shocked M.R. Jayakar in 1925 was not the outburst of a man embittered by suffering. The experience only aggravated traits that ever dwelt within him – a yearning for sheer revenge and a lust for human blood. Without doubt, then, *The First Indian War of Independence – 1857* merits close analysis.

Savarkar was obsessed with the past. He wrote in the introduction to *Indian War of Independence*:

> The nation that has no consciousness of its past has no future. Equally true it is that a nation must develop its capacity not only of claiming a past but also of knowing

> how to use it for the furtherance of its future. The nation ought to be the master and not the slave of its own history. For, it is absolutely unwise to try certain things now irrespective of special considerations, simply because they had been once acted in the past. The feeling of hatred against the Mahomedans was just and necessary in the times of Shivaji – but, such a feeling would be unjust and foolish if nursed now, simply because it was the dominant feeling of the Hindus then. One must distil principles from history rather than treat it as mere narrative.[4]

He excelled Asoka Mehta in praising the Muslims for their role in 1857. Here, again, he wants to detect principle in the narrative:

> What were they that Moulvies preached them, learned Brahmins blessed them, that for their success prayers went up to Heaven from the Mosques of Delhi and the Temples of Benares? The great principles were Swadharma and Swaraj. In the thundering roar of 'Din, Din,' which rose to protect religion, when there were evident signs of a cunning, dangerous and destructive attack on religion dearer than life, and in the terrific blows dealt at the chain of slavery with the holy desire of acquiring Swaraj [so that] the principles of Swadharma and Swaraj will be embedded in the bone and marrow of all the sons of Hindustan! (p. 8)

Here, 'Hindustan' is used very much in the same sense as was used by the great Muhammad Iqbal in his famous poem: '*Saare jahan se accha Hindustan hamara*' ('Our Hindustan is the best among all the countries of the world').

There was generous praise for the last Mughal Emperor Bahadur Shah Zafar and most of all for 'that patriot Moulvie Ahmad Shah, whose sacred name has cast a halo round Hindusthan. . . . As soon as the news of his death reached England, the relieved Englishmen felt that the most formidable enemy of the British in Northern India was no more.' In support of this assertion he cited

Holmes's *History of the Indian Mutiny* (p. 539). Sarvarkar spared himself no pains.

Claims to greatness of Hyder Ali and Tipu Sultan were not overlooked, either. 'The danger to the Independence of India was first perceived by Nana Farnavis of Poona and Hyder Sahib of Mysore. . . . The Gadi of Tanjore, the Masnad of Mysore, the Raigarh of Sahyadri, the Dewan-I-khas of Delhi were among the select actors' in the drama that was unfolding in India (pp. 13–14).

The feeling is unmistakable: *Indian War of Independence* was written by a man proud of his religious and cultural heritage, proud of Maharashtra's past and yet someone who sought to blend regional and religious loyalties together in a over-arching loyalty to the Indian nation. Interestingly, there is an entire chapter devoted to Ayodhya (chapter IV). This chapter, however, contains none of the falsehoods retailed by his political heirs of today. The message, throughout, is one of national unity.

Nana Sahib, son of Baji Rao, had the brilliant Azimullah Khan as his trusted emissary, the author noted. One gets a good idea of Savarkar's outlook at the time from this passage:

> Nana's programme was first to fight a united fight, to make India free and, by removing internecine warfare, to establish *the rule of the United States of India* which would, thus, take its rightful place in the council of the free nations of the earth. He, also, felt that the meaning of 'Hindusthan' was thereafter the united nation of the adherents of Islam as well as Hinduism. As long as the Mahomedans lived in India in the capacity of the alien rulers, so long, to be willing to live with them like brothers was to acknowledge national weakness. Hence, it was, upto then, necessary for the Hindus to consider the Mahomedans as foreigners. And moreover this rulership of the Mahomedans, Guru Govind in the Punjab, Rana Pratap in Rajputana, Chatrasal in Bundelkhand, and the Mahrattas by even sitting upon the throne at Delhi, had destroyed, and after a struggle of centuries, Hindu sovereignty had defeated the rulership of

> the Mahomedans and had come to its own all over India. *It was no national shame to join hands with Mahomedans then, but it would, on the contrary, be an act of generosity.*
>
> *So, now, the antagonism between the Hindus and the Mahomedans might be consigned to the past.* Their present relation was one not of rulers and ruled, foreigner and native, but simply that of *brothers,* with the one difference between them of religion alone. For, they were both children of the soil of Hindusthan. Their names were different, but they were all children of the same Mother. India, therefore, being the common mother of these two, they were brothers by blood. Nana Sahib, Bahadur Shah of Delhi, Moulvi Ahmad Shah, Khan Bahadur Khan, and other leaders of 1857 felt this relationship to some extent and, so, gathered round the flag of Swadesh leaving aside their enmity, now so unreasonable and stupid. In short, the broad features of the policy of Nana Sahib and Azimullah were that the Hindus and the Mahomedans should unite and fight shoulder to shoulder for the independence of their country and that, when freedom was gained, the United States of India should be formed under the Indian rulers and princes. (pp. 59–60)

He keeps returning to this theme of unity between Hindus and Muslims and keeps emphasizing that in the struggle for independence, the two must act as brothers.

> These five days [in Delhi] will be ever memorable in the history of Hindusthan for yet another reason. Because these five days proclaimed by beat of drum the end for the time being at any rate of the continuous fight between the Hindus and Mahomedans dating from the invasion of Mohammed of Ghazni. It was proclaimed first that the Hindus and the Mahomedans are not rivals, not conquerors and the conquered, but brethren: Bharatmata (Mother India) who was, in times past, freed from Mahomedan [sic] yoke by

> Shivaji, Pratap Singh, Chattrasal, Pratapaditya, Guru Govind Singh, and Mahadaji Scindia – that Bharatmata gave the sacred mandate that day. Henceforward you are equal and brothers, I am equally the mother of you both! The five days during which Hindus and Mahomedans proclaimed that India was their country and that they were all brethren, the days when Hindus and Mahomedans unanimously raised the flat of national freedom at Delhi. Be those grand days ever memorable in the history of Hindusthan! (pp. 99–100)

There was praise for 'the Crescent of the Islamites' as much as for 'the spears of the Mahratthas' (p. 78). The Mughals had come and ruled as foreign conquerors. 1857 consigned that to the past. Bahadur Shah was acclaimed as the King by all Indians. In a passage that bared, both his hopes for the future and memories of a past with all its imagined wrongs he wrote:

> The Mogul dynasty of old was not chosen by the people of the land. It was thrust upon India by sheer force, dignified by the name of conquest, and upheld by a powerful pack of alien adventurers and native self-seekers. It was not this throne that was restored to Bahadur Shah today. No, that would have been impossible, for, such thrones are conquered and not received. That would have been suicidal, for then, it would have been in vain that the blood of hundreds of Hindu martyrs had been shed in the three or four centuries preceding.
>
> From the death of Prithvi Raj right up to the death of Aurangzeb, the war was without a truce. And in the midst of this gory struggle of countless years, a Hindu power arose in the western mountains of Bharat Varsha, which was destined to fulfill the mission of the innumerable dead, who fell fighting in protecting the honour of the race. From out of Poona, a Hindu Prince Bhausahib – advanced with a mighty host, captured the throne of Delhi, and vindicated the honour of the Hindu civilization, the conqueror was

> conquered and India was again free, the blot of slavery and defeat being wiped off. Hindus again were masters of the land of the Hindus.
>
> So, in the truer sense, we said that the raising of Bahadur Shah to the throne of India was no restoration at all. *But rather it was the declaration that the longstanding war between the Hindu and the Mahomedan had ended, that tyranny had ceased.* . . . Let, then, Hindus and Mahomedans send forth their hearty, conscientious, and most loyal homage to this elected or freely accepted Emperor of their native soil on the 11th of May, 1857! (pp. 225–26)

Not only Muslim personalities but Muslim masses indeed even 'the mullahs' receive high praise: 'Also among the vast Mussalman population of the town, the Mullahs were very busy. Thousands of Mussalmans were only awaiting the signal with a firm determination to offer their blood on the battle-field in the cause of country and religion.'

Savarkar was writing of the past. But his admonitions were clearly meant for the future.

> The Englishmen will try now also their old work of deception, they will try to incite the Hindus to rise against Mussalmans, and the Mahomedans to rise against the Hindus. But, Hindu Brethren! Do not fall into their nets. It is hardly necessary to tell our clever Hindu Brethren that the English never keep their promises . . . .
>
> Mussalmans, if you revere the Koran, and Hindus, if you revere the cow-mother, forget now your minor differences and unite together in this sacred war! Jump into the battlefield fighting under one banner, and wash away the name of the English from India in streams of blood! If the Hindus will join hands with the Mahomedans in this war, if they will also take the field for the freedom of our country, then, as a reward for their patriotism, the killing of cows will be put a stop to. (pp. 140–41)

### The propensity to violence

Misconceptions about the past were bad enough. What is more disturbing is the exposure of Savarkar's psyche. Note how easily Savarkar approves of violence and bloodletting.

> So long as that divine age has not arrived, so long as the highly auspicious end remains only in the lines of saintly poets and in the prophecies of the divinely inspired, and so long as, even to make that state of universal justice possible, the human mind has to be busy eradicating sinful and aggressive tendencies, so long, rebellion, *bloodshed, and revenge cannot be purely sinful.* As long as the word 'rule' is used for 'authority' both just and unjust, so long its antonym 'rebellion' can, also, be just as well as unjust. . . . *Revolt, bloodshed and revenge have often been instruments created by nature to root out injustice and introduce an era of justice.* And when justice uses these terrible means for her salvation, the blame of it does not lie on justice but on the preceding cruel injustice. . . .
>
> And it was the fire of such a divine vengeance that was burning in the heart of the sons of Hindusthan in 1857. Their thrones were broken, their crowns smashed, their country taken away, their religions trodden under foot, their lands confiscated, their properties robbed, and laws despised, they had been cheated with promise made only to be broken, insults and outrages had reached a climax ... Life itself had lost all its charms for them on account of the dire dishonour in which they had sunk. Requests were in vain, so also, were petitions, complaints, wailings, and cries, all in vain. Then the natural reaction began and everywhere could be heard the whispers of '*Revenge*'. India had been subjected to innumerable, cruel oppressions each of which, individually, would have justified the revenge. If there had been no revolution even after all this, we would have had to say 'India is dead!' . . .

> [Such vengeance is justified] indeed if there was no propensity in human nature towards a terrible revenge for an horrible injustice suffered, the brute in man would have been still the dominating factor in human dealings. Is not one of the most important functions of law – the punishment of crime? (pp. 217–19)

In the evening of his life Savarkar wrote an altogether different 'history'. But it was laced with the same emotion of revenge.[5] *The Six Glorious Epoch* was India's independence from British rule. It makes sad reading. Tipu Sultan is dubbed 'The Savage'. Names for the rest can be easily imagined. Referring to his book *Indian War of Independence*, he wrote, 'In it I have reviewed that war *from the standpoint of the Hindu nation*';[6] the role of the Muslims in the revolt is suppressed. The Muslims, according to Savarkar, eventually got what they wanted: 'The British Statesmen insisted that India be vivisected into two because they wanted to reward those *Muslims who had consistently and treacherously helped the British throughout the Indian War of Liberation ever since 1857*, and who demanded a unified state of the Muslim-majority provinces cut out from the rest of India, as a price for that help.'

This roll call of villains is not without its heroes though. The Hindu Mahasabha alone, we are told, opposed India's partition. 'Throughout the whole of India these avowed pro-Hindu (Hindutva-nishtas) faced boldly all the atrocities of the enemies, even when they were in a minority. They even did not refrain from *avenging the spilling of Hindu blood by shedding the enemy blood and by beheading those who proved treacherous to the Hindu cause.*' It is blood, blood all the time.

However, one must assess each of the two books in its own context and on its own merits. Subhoranjan Dasgupta is absolutely correct when he says that

> It is difficult to quote Savarkar's statements on Indian history out of context because the context itself is drastically vitiated. In his *The Six Glorious Epochs,* which is regarded as the bible by RSS pracharaks, Emperor Asoka is accused of gross

> intolerance towards Vedantic Hindus. Tipu Sultan, in his words, was a barbaric Sultan who was mercifully vanquished by the Marathas and the British. And Muslim Akbar had to be 'foreign, cruel, intolerant and bidharmi'.

His version of history is also determined to interpret Buddhism and Sikhism as integral branches of Hinduism though Buddhists and Sikhs see themselves as being distinct from Hindus. Dasgupta hits the hammer on the nail when he notes that

> Lastly, while offering homage to Hindu martyr Vir Banda Bairagi in the same book, this ageless nationalist rejoices at 'the most appropriate retaliation of the molestation of the Hindu women'. The retaliation took the form of 'the burning of the Muslim locality . . . not to speak of the subject parade of Muslim men, women and children, bare-footed, in the hot sun . . . and finally the proclamation of a Hindu state in the whole of the Punjab.

This is Savarkar's theory and practice of 'super-atrocious reprisals'. And this is the man the BJP and the Sangh *parivar* holds up as an icon, an example. How deep their admiration for him is can be gauged when one replaces Punjab with Gujarat in the above passage. This is the man Advani honoured on the holy land of Andaman island on May 4, 2002.

# 3 ANDAMANS AND THE ORIGINS OF HINDUTVA

SAVARKAR WAS NOT the only one to be consigned to the horrors of the Cellular Jail in the Andaman Islands. He suffered grievously, as, indeed, all the other prisoners did. This is not to belittle him, just to place facts on record. No one reading his account can withhold sympathy and compassion.[1] He was yoked to an oil mill. So, indeed, were some others as Prof. R.C. Majumdar's work, based on archival material reveals.[2]

He was brought to the Andamans on July 4, 1911. Soon thereafter, in that very year, he was on his knees pleading for clemency. The text of this petition and its date are not available. It is however referred to in his Petition of November 24, 1913. Neither of these petitions is mentioned in his letters home. His health had not broken down then. Only the spirit had crumbled. As it tended to, rather too readily, whenever he was faced with the consequences of the wrongs he had instigated others to commit. His health began to decline in 1915–16, and finally broke down in 1918. He wrote to his brother on August 4, 1918, 'So far as to the advantages in the jail [after being promoted to the second class]; but all this was bearable to me when my health was comparatively sound. But this year I must tell you that great and counting [sic] disadvantage has been added to my lot for my health is utterly broken.'[3] But, as we shall see, he so managed to ingratiate himself with the authorities that he, a 'dangerous' inmate, was made foreman. Few revolutionaries would have accepted this 'honour' from their captives who were also rulers of their captive land.

### Assessing Savarkar

Savarkar's suffering should not be underplayed. But neither should the enormity of his surrenders and compromises. Those who hail him as a hero exaggerate the first and explain away, when they cannot deny, the second. Subhoranjan Dasgupta puts the matter in proper perspective.

> Vinayak Damodar Savarkar was of course a freedom fighter. . . . Neither did he die fighting the British like some of the veer revolutionaries who led the Chittagong Uprising nor did he opt defiant martyrdom like Bhagat Singh and Khudiram.
>
> After brave struggle in the first decade of the last century, his spirit crumbled to such an extent that he pleaded for mercy more than once. . . . Many other revolutionaries tortured in the Cellular Jail of Andamans could not dream of seeking similar mercy.

Veer Savarkar did. And by addressing the colonial oppressor as 'mighty and merciful', he initiated the RSS tradition of abject co-operation with the British. What began with him ended on a much more jarring note in the turbulent forties. Little wonder, then, that the Indian Council of Historical Research (ICHR) governed by that Savarkar acolyte, Murli Manohar Joshi, thwarted the publication of two volumes of the *Towards Freedom* series[4] which exposes this later complicity with the help of irrefutable documents.

The seeds of the Sangh *parivar's* collaboration with the British rulers were sown by this 'revolutionary' in 1911–13. The record of his offer to Viceroy Linlithgow, on October 9, 1939, shows how low he was prepared to stoop, and at a time when the Congress had decided to quit the ministries in the provinces as a prelude to renewal of the struggle against the British.

The first Marathi edition of *The Story of My Transportation for Life* was published in 1927. It was proscribed before long. The ban was lifted in 1947. The book is full of communal hate. His earlier book on 1857 had argued that the Hindus and Muslims must come together to oust the British. When and where did the change in Savarkar's outlook come about? It is difficult to ascertain this with any degree of certainty. But it can be argued that there was, in fact, no sharp break from the past. For, as we saw in the previous chapter, a communal view of India's history was evident in his book on 1857. It must be borne in mind that while Savarkar was in the Andamans, a hero to the world, virtually no one was aware of his the surrender to the British. Even his communal worldview and hatred of Muslims was not very well known. His surrender was due to an instant collapse of morale. The petitions of 1911 and 1913 surfaced after his death when the archives were consulted. Given the image of a 'revolutionary', the public took an indulgent view of the undertakings he gave in 1924, which the government published. But apparently neither the extra document – the certificate he so enthusiastically gave on the fairness of his trial – nor the apologies he frantically tendered when he was rapped on the wrist for communal propaganda were published. Only by the mid-twenties did his communalist outlook become known.

### Communal propaganda in prison

It would be too much to assert that ill treatment by Muslim warders in jail shaped Savarkar's communal outlook. Other prisoners suffered no such change in outlook especially when he claims that 'all political prisoners had Mussalmans for their warders' and 'the Hindus suffered doubly. First from their fellow-prisoners, the Muslims and secondly from their Muslim warders' (pp. 90–91). The entire second chapter of the book is devoted to 'The "*Shuddhi*" movement in the Andamans'. His language is coarse.

> If it is a foolish waste of time and a childish pursuit to retain in Hinduism those born in it, may be, sinners, criminals and the miscreants of society, how can one explain the Muslim campaign, now going on for a thousand years, to win this riff-raff, condemned class of Hindu society for Islam? The Mussalmans have waged wars for it, they have put men and women to the sword, they have burnt and looted houses

> – in short they have declared Jehad – for effecting this mass conversion. (pp. 282–83)

He complains that 'we as Hindus have lost terribly for not playing the game which others have played' (p. 286). Savarkar 'played' it inside the prison as well as outside it, he claimed, through convicts assigned to duty with the people outside in the settlement. 'From the prison the *Shuddhi* movement began to spread outwards among the free inhabitants of the Andamans' (p. 312). The campaign was begun shortly after his arrival.

> I began my work of *Shuddhi* in the year 1913 and fought my first battle in its favour in the same year. From that date to 1920–21, I did that work in the Andamans, from 1921–24, I continued it in my prison-days in India, and from my release in 1924, I have been pursuing it to this day. And I have invariably carried it on in the interest of freedom, justice and fair-play for all. I have no hatred in my heart for the Christian, the Mussalman, and the heathen, or for those whom they style as primitive barbarians. I do not look down upon any one of them with scorn and contempt. I only oppose that section of it vehemently, which is oppressive and violent towards another. For I believe firmly that the *Shuddhi* movement itself will build a bridge of permanent union between the Hindus and the Muslims, and will bring good to both and lasting advantage to India as a whole. (p. 326)

This is convoluted logic, if ever there was any. How on earth the so-called *shuddhi* can bring about 'permanent union' between various communities is hard to fathom.

### Surrender and compromise

Turkey supported Germany in the First World War, which began in 1914. This is how Savarkar saw the situation:

> The siding of Turkey with Germany as against England, roused all my suspicions about Pan-Islamism and I scented in that move a danger to India. I discovered that Turkey in this war had made it possible for Germany to stretch her long arm to India and create a critical situation in India itself. This was, indeed, a circumstance favourable to my designs. For then England was bound to grant India all the rights that she would demand, or India herself could wrest them as the result of exhaustion of England and Germany both, battered as they would be in this terrible combat between two mighty foes, not unlike the fight of two powerful elephants . . . joined in life-and-death struggle with each other. Broken, battered, bleeding and exhausted they will lie on the field with victory to neither, and with full advantage to others who knew to profit by the situation. But I also fear that in this grim struggle between two mighty powers *the Muslims in India might find their devil's opportunity to invite the Muslim hordes from the North to ravage in that effort by the machinations in Russia.* (p. 339)

In all this, Savarkar saw a chance for himself.

> Thinking calmly over all these near and remote consequences of the war, I settled my own line of action, and, as the beginning of it, I resolved to send a long letter on the subject to the Government of India. I cannot here give my reader what line of action I had settled in my mind to follow. But I may summarise in outline the letter I had sent to the Government of India. The Suprintendent agreed to forward the letter and I wrote in it as follows: I wrote that I felt it my duty and intimately connected with the revolutionary movement in India, what I thought about the present situation in India vis-à-vis the war between England and Germany.

The terms of his offer bear quotation in full:

> Let the Government give us a chance to prove our bona fides. Let them release us to convince the people that England was willing to break the chains that had held India in thrall. We pledged our word of honour that we would exert our utmost to bring recruits to the Indian Army in large numbers that would equip her to stave off the invasion of India from the North by forces of Afghanistan and Turkey, and to march to any front that needed her presence to fight the foe and beat him. We would offer ourselves as volunteers to serve in that army in defence of India and for the victory of England. Release us, I said, equip India with colonial self-government, and win the loyalty and love of her people. That would assure to Government all the co-operation that it needed from the people in the present crisis. Let it not miss that splendid opportunity.

One has only to compare this with the text of his abject letter of November 14, 1913 concerning his own release to realise that this could not be all that he wrote. Ottoman Turkey joined Germany and Austria as a belligerent ally on October 31, 1914.[5] Savarkar renewed his offer when the news reached the Andamans. He records that there was a great deal of eagerness among the prisoners for news of war, 'although I knew that it had no deeper root in their heart than the selfish [sic] longing to be free' (pp. 344–45). Note the hypocrisy here: Savarkar himself was trying his best to strike a deal with the authorities for his release or at least for better conditions (for himself, not for all prisoners) in prison, but if others sought release from prison, they were branded 'selfish'.

Savarkar did manage to get for himself better conditions. He was appointed a foreman and he used this to lord over the Muslim prisoners:

> The Mussalmans had been, therefore, fully aware, when I became a foreman, what I expected of them, that I was particularly proud of the Hindu way of greeting and of the

> words used along with that greeting like 'Rama Rama', 'Namaskar', 'Bande mataram', so on and so forth. The Mussalmans full of tremor at my appointment as the head of the oil depot were anxious to conciliate me at any cost. (p. 496)

He also used his appointment more profitably. He appointed 'Hindu warders in place of those' he dismissed. 'My office as the foreman of the oil-depot was, of course, of great use to me in furthering the movements of *Shuddhi, Sanghat* and education started for an all-round improvement in the Andamans' (p. 499). He also began propagating Hindi as the national language, but unlike Gandhi,[6] his advocacy of Hindi involved a hatred of Urdu.

> As we learn German so we may learn Urdu. But as mother-tongue and national language it had no place in Hindu culture. . . . The Andamans which knew no other language than Urdu, and where Hindu girls talking to each other spontaneously uttered the word '*shadi*' to indicate marriage and knew not its Sanskrit or Hindi equivalent, now saw a transformation that was indeed, a miracle. (pp. 492–93)

He considered Urdu a threat to Hindi: 'for the last forty years' Keer wrote in 1950, Savarkar held that 'Urdu should be preserved for Muslims'.[7] On this, as on many issues, Savarkar's illiteracy was astounding. It is well known that Urdu has been enriched by Hindu writers and poets no less than by Muslims. 'Savarkar held that if the importance and the future of the Andamans was to be increased usefully in reference to the safety and predominance of Hindustan and Hindu culture, Hindi and Nagari should be made compulsory in the Andamans'.[8] Till the Partition, in fact, Urdu was commonly used all over north India. Bhagat Singh wrote to his brother in Urdu; the FIR on Gandhi's murder was recorded by the police in Urdu.

The annals of the Cellular Jail in the Andamans record no other conversion of a nationalist to communalism, no other complaints of Muslims wardens ill-treating Hindu inmates. Savarkar's 'conversion' was less sharp a break from his past when read alongside his communal view of Indian history. Imaginary complaints were a consistent feature of his justification for his ideology.

Savarkar met the Home Member of the Government of India, Reginald Craddock in October 1913 shortly before he wrote his letter of November 14, 1913. Letters to his brother Narayan are not illuminating on these moves. The letter of March 9, 1915 urges Narayan to promote a public petition for release. Omitted altogether is mention of his own letter of November 1913. There is no mention of his clemency petition of 1911 either in his first letter of December 15, 1912, or of the interview with Craddock in his letter of February 15, 1914. Only the letter of August 4, 1918, mentions Savarkar's petition to the Secretary of State for India, Edwin S. Montagu, apparently in October 1911.

> I had put before Mr Montagu and the Viceroy a frank statement of the case of such an amnesty as this. The main points being that while they were considering the question of the Reforms in India they should not fail to recognize that if they aimed at the establishment of any responsible Government in India they should thereby render it utterly futile to continue to lock us in jail.

### Conduct in prison

R.C. Majumdar's book *Penal Statement in Andamans* provides a fuller and documented account based on the archives. Majumdar accepts Savarkar's version uncritically in most instances,[9] except on an episode which proved too much even for his credulity. As Prof. Mushirul Hasan points out, 'K.M. Munshi and R.C. Majumdar, editors of the Bhartiya Vidya Bhawan series, mostly echoed the rhetoric of Hindu extremist politics, tracing the misfortunes of Bharat to centuries of tyrannical Muslim rule. Instead of studying and interpreting other cultures as their own, without prejudice or even trimmed to serve some non-scholarly purpose, whether religious or regional or ideological or other.'[10]

Majumdar's narrative, as we said above, draws mostly on Savarkar's version. Savarkar's account is a characteristically varnished one (pp. 247–50). Even so, this bit in Savarkar's own account is revealing:

> I may tell you [Craddock], however, that it is entirely in your hands to take me out of this. Mr Gokhale has just brought in his resolution on compulsory education in the Imperial Legislative Council. If it is accepted by Government, and if such measures of progress are assured to my people that they may rise as a nation, then not only myself but all my friends who are dubbed as revolutionaries will be ready to turn to the path of peace. They must be thinking similarly, I feel sure, as I am speaking to you now.

Savarkar was prepared to clutch at any straw. The relevance of a law on education to the goals of a 'revolutionary' is not very evident. Five years later in 1918, Savarkar lauded the Montagu-Chelmsford Reforms (named after the Secretary of State and the Viceroy) which no 'revolutionary' could have accepted. He offered to support the reforms,

> If the reforms whole heartedly effected and worked out by the Government would serve the purpose of such a constitutional breach as that then revolution ceases and evolution becomes a watchword and a rallying cry of us all. And I as one humble soldier in Her rank would honestly try my best to make the reform successful, that is, work them out so as to render them a stepping stone to the realization of the great mission of our generation of making India free and great and glorious, leading or marching hand in and with others to the appointed destiny of man. (p. 490)

Majumdar writes, 'Savarkar has reproduced in his book at some length the gist of his conversation with him [Craddock in 1913] which shows that while *Savarkar had changed his views, the Government view remained the same as before.*'[11] On his return to Delhi, Craddock recorded the following:

> Savarkar's petition is one for mercy. He cannot be said to express any regret or repentance, but he affects to have changed his views, urging that the hopeless condition of Indians in 1906–1907 was his excuse for entering upon a conspiracy. Since that time, he said, the Government had shown itself much more conciliatory in the matter of councils, education and so forth, that the case for revolutionary action had disappeared. Mercy to him would, he said, have a calming effect upon those who still conspire against the British rule, and he was willing and anxious to send an open letter to the native press explaining his change of views. He admitted that he had no legal rights in the matter but pleaded for merciful consideration, and asked for a transfer to a jail in India or Burma where he would at least gain the moral right to be released after fourteen years. He pressed me hard to give some promise, or to record something that would give him hope, true or false, that his case would be considered later on. I pointed out to him that a mere statement of change of views could not wipe out his record, and that apart from the purely political aspect of his case, he had been convicted of abetment of murder in the case of Mr Jackson of Nasik. He had been instrumental in sending out 20 Browning pistols. He explained that the pistols were not intended for murder but in furtherance of a revolutionary movement. When I pointed out to him that revolutions could not be carried out by pistols, and that pistols could only be used for murder, he was unable to give any answer. . . . I could only therefore advise him to seek such alleviations as life in the jail could afford him by conforming to prison discipline and from the books to which he was allowed access.[12]

Despite his own moves to secure release and the fact that he had won concessions as a foreman, Savarkar wrote contemptuously of others who had won concessions. These political prisoners, he claimed, were at the 'beck and call for anything they [the authorities] needed', and 'became very subservient – not to put it more bluntly – to the authorities' (p. 257). This is too much for even an admirer like Majumdar to take: 'This is a very serious insinuation against these political prisoners and we have no means to determine how far Savarkar was justified in this assumption. He does not give any evidence or practical illustration.'[13]

On another question, of a strike by the prisoners, Majumdar records that

> an interesting account of the prison life in Cellular Jail during the period from 1916 to 1920 is given by one Trailokya Nath Chakravarti, generally known as Maharaj, a redoubtable revolutionary leader who passed away in Delhi on August 9, 1970. He was in the Andamans from 1916 to 1921. Chakravarti alleged in his memoirs *Jele Tirish Bochor* (Thirty Years in Jail) published in 1938 that Savarkar and his brother Ganpat, who was also there, secretly encouraged him and others to call a strike but did not join it.

To Majumdar this is an 'uncharitable aspersion'. He reproduces Savarkar's explanation.

> If I were to openly lead them, Mr Barrie and the authorities over him would get the opportunity they needed to take off all the concessions which had come to me and old political prisoners according to jail rules, and would put me back in solitary confinement. . . . Hence it was the young and the energetic among us to shoulder the burden, and these hundred and odd persons must by turns keep up the agitation and all the activities connected with it. The last and the most important reasons for my abstaining from it was that I would have forfeited thereby my right of sending a letter to India. It was a rule that a letter was allowed to be sent annually by one whose record during the year was clear of any punishment. If I were punished or went on strike, my right would go along with it, and to be deprived of my right was not only to harm the strike, but, more important

> than that, to lose the chance of working for the freedom of the political prisoners themselves.

This does not repel Majumdar. On the contrary, it arouses the historian's admiration:

> Whatever one may think of the explanation, it is difficult not to be deeply impressed by the candour and sincerity of the great patriotic leader. How far the younger generation of the political prisoners was impressed by it, it is difficult to say, but the comments of Chakravarti indicate that at least one section was not quite satisfied. In any case, the younger groups stuck to their programme and continued the general strike.

Majumdar quotes Savarkar's own testimony on how prisoners much older – and braver – than him went on a hunger strike.

> One of them was the sixty-year old Sikh political prisoner, Sardar Sohan Singh. The other was a spirited Rajput young man from Punjab, named Prithvi Singh. For twelve days they lay confined in the prison cell without a morsel of food. At last, the authorities had to yield and admit their written statement, which embodied all the grievances of the strikers. . . . As their statement was received by the authorities, the Sikh Sohan Singh called off the strike, but Prithvi Singh continued for two weeks more.[14]

The contrast between a true revolutionary and a fake one is glaring. The record of Savarkar's stay in the Andamans is an unedifying one. Yet, more – and worse – was to follow when, eventually, he was shifted to the Ratnagiri Jail. He gave the disgraceful undertakings of January 6, 1924. Thus was revealed to the public then the glimpse of a trait, which archival discoveries revealed years later in all its hideousness.

# 4 HINDUTVA VS HINDUISM

'You can tell a man who boozes by the company he chooses': goes the opening of one of Benjamin Burt's songs. A political party, punch drunk with power, is judged by the man it lauds as its hero in the moments of its inebriation.

Savarkar was not a religious fundamentalist at all. He was what the historian Bipan Chandra termed 'a practicing atheist'.[1] *Savarkar was not interested in religion.* The religious fundamentalist misinterprets his religion and perverts its message to secure his political ends.[2] Savarkar did not *misinterpret* Hinduism. He ignored it. He did not pervert the message of religion to serve the ends of his politics. He perverted history for use in the service of his politics, a politics based on manufactured ancient wrongs for the spread of hatred and the spirit of revenge.

Inevitably, the yatra which Savarkar's devotee L.K. Advani launched in 1990 in a self-proclaimed crusade for Hindutva ended on December 6, 1992, with the demolition of the Babri Masjid. The BJP leader Sushma Swaraj ripped apart all pretence, in Bhopal on April 14, 2000 when she admitted that the Ram Janmabhoomi movement was 'purely political in nature and had nothing to do with religion'.[3]

What does Hindutva mean, precisely? And, what does it spell for the people of India? Hindutva is not against the interests of only the minorities. The outlook, prospect and lives of millions of Hindus will be blighted by it. It is certainly not synonymous with Hinduism. The 1996 election manifesto of the BJP speaks of 'Hindutva or *cultural* nationalism'. This is in rejection of what Savarkar and the RSS Chief Golwalkar called 'territorial nationalism'. This was the kind of nationalism known the would over and which the Indian National Congress espoused since its birth: every one born in the territory of India is an Indian by birth. Gandhi and Nehru enriched this concept. Implicit in it is the concept of India's secularism, democracy and its 'composite culture'. We are one nation with cultures as diverse as our land itself, yet knit together by a common loyalty to India.

Consistently with its rejection of this 'territorial nationalism', the BJP rejects the concept of a 'composite culture' also. The BJP election manifesto (1996 as well as 1998) declared, 'The BJP believes in one nation, one people, one culture'. That 'one culture' which it flaunts is the heart of its 'cultural nationalism'. The reader could not have failed to discern its import by now – it is *Hindu* nationalism. The 1998 Manifesto is more explicit in the section, 'Our National Identity, Cultural Nationalism'. It says, plainly enough, that 'the cultural nationalism of India . . . is the core of Hindutva'.

Not surprisingly, it firmly links the Ayodhya movement to this ideology. 'It is with such integrative ideas in mind, the BJP joined the Ram Janmabhoomi movement for the construction of Shri Ram Mandir at Ayodhya.... Shri Ram lies at the core of Indian consciousness.'

This movement was begun by the VHP on August 19, 1984. It was set up by the RSS in Mumbai for this very purpose.[4] The BJP formally joined the movement on June 11, 1989, when at Palampur its National Executive adopted a resolution on the issue demanding that the 'Ram Janmasthan [be] handed over to the Hindus'. This was probably the first time in independent India that a major political party had taken a partisan, communal line. For the BJP it was par for the course.

Elections to the Lok Sabha were only a few months away. On this very issue, the BJP brought down the National Front government headed by Vishwanath Pratap Singh in 1990. L.K. Advani embarked on his blood-drenched rath yatra. He said, on September 24, 1990, on the eve of the Somnath-Ayodhya rath yatra: 'ideologically, I am ranged against all political parties because of this issue. All political parties think alike'. The issue was clearly defined. It was not Ram Janambhoomi. It was a 'crusade in defence of Hindutva and a crusade against pseudo-secularism'. The movement reached its climax with the demolition of the Babri Masjid on December 6, 1992. However, BJP's election manifestos of 1996 and 1998, not to forget the utterances of its mentor, the RSS, suggest that its real goal is not limited to the Ayodhya campaign. It is to recast Indian polity thoroughly and replace the spirit and ethos of Indian nationalism with the exclusionary and poisonous credo of Hindutva. The real goal, then, is to establish a Hindu Rashtra. The Constitution will retain its husk, denuded of its democratic liberal and secular content. The ideological guidance here, as in much else, comes from Savarkar.

### Swarajya and Hindutva

Decades ago Savarkar warned the Hindus not to be misled by the Congress concept of freedom:

> Mere geographical independence of the bit of earth called India should not be confused with real 'Swarajya'. To the Hindus, the independence of Hindusthan could only be worth having if it ensured 'their Hindutva – their religious, racial and cultural identity', Swarajya to the Hindus must mean only that 'Rajya' in which their 'Swatva', their 'Hindutva' could assert itself without being overloaded by non-Hindu people, whether they be Indian territorials or extraterritorials.[5]

One of his followers said that Hindus

> cannot take this country as jointly owned by those who either came running away from their countries and sought protection here or those descendants of ex-Hindus, who for the greed of power and money or out of fear renounced their glorious faith and became converts, or those who are

> the descendants of those barbarous invaders who spoiled our very sacred land, demolished our sacred temples . . . the country cannot belong to them, if they are to live here, they must live here taking it for granted that Hindusthan is the land of the Hindus, of no one else.[6]

Savarkar's followers like Advani and Vajpayee are less candid, but no less committed. They denounce Nehru but the real target is Gandhi. Nehru was his devoted disciple and the man Gandhi himself anointed as his heir. Godse's bullet killed Gandhi. Savarkar and the various fronts of the Sangh *parivar* seek to bury the Gandhian heritage which Nehru lovingly fostered and enriched over the years. A veritable campaign of 'cultural assassination' is now afoot in the name of 'cultural nationalism'. This baleful campaign draws its inspiration from Savarkar's essay *Hindutva* published in 1923 under the pseudonym 'A Maratha' since he was in prison.[7]

Savarkar died a political failure. He and his Hindu Mahasabha had ceased to be players in Indian politics since the early forties. But his ideology took new life once it was adopted by the RSS in its entire nuance. It is writ large in Golwalkar's book *We or Our Nationhood Defined* (1938). Vajpayee was wrong in saying in the Rajya Sabha in May 6, 2002 that the book represented Golwalkar's personal views.[8] The book was cited in a formal legal document filed in 1978 before the District Judge, Nagpur by the RSS, *as an organization.*[9] Keer records that in a speech in Mumbai on May 15, 1963 Golwalkar said that 'he found the principles of nationalism scientifically explained in Savarkar's great work *Hindutva.* To him it was a text-book, a scientific book'.[10] It was on this occasion that Golwalkar also publicly acknowledged his debt to the book *Rashtra Meemansa* by Savarkar's elder brother Babarao (G.D.) Savarkar. Golwalkar's own *Bunch of Thoughts*[11] reflects a deep impress of Hindutva. It has a whole chapter denouncing 'Territorial Nationalism'. It was also relied on by the RSS in the 1978 document. Golwalkar himself acknowledged that 'Veer Savarkarji wrote a beautiful book "Hindutva" and Hindu Mahasabha based itself on that pure philosophy of *Hindu Nationalism.*'[12] This is precisely what

Advani began advocating in 1990, and the BJP in its election manifestos since 1996. The true originator of this philosophy, Savarkar, was himself hailed only in 2002.

This long neglect of their intellectual guide by the Sangh *parivar* was commented upon with remarkable perception by Swapan Dasgupta, himself an admirer of Hindutva. This is what he wrote in the aftermath of the demolition of the Babari Masjid:

> Savarkar's abysmal failure in the realms of realpolitik is more than compensated by his continuing relevance as the chief theoretician of modern Hindu nationalism. Neither the RSS nor the BJP has highlighted this aspect sufficiently, preferring to emphasize its intellectual lineage from Bankim Chandra Chatterjee, Swami Vivekananda, Swami Dayananda, Lokmanya Tilak and Sri Aurobindo right down to Guruji [sic] Golwalkar and Deendayal Upadhyaya. It is, however, a commentary on Savarkar's perspicacity that his celebrated pamphlet, *Hindutva*, written in 1923, remains the starting point of any theoretical construct of the Hindu upsurge.
>
> . . . Just as he attempted to rescue Hindutva from the Hindu penchant for spiritual abstractions, Savarkar was equally categorical in defining nationhood. 'A Hindu', he wrote in a celebrated definition, 'means a person who regards this land of Bharatavarsha from the Indus to the seas as his fatherland (*pitribhumi*), as well as his holyland (*punyabhumi*), that is the cradle land of his religion.
>
> It is surprising that for a man who flaunted his irreverence and rationalism, Savarkar attached so much importance to formal religion in defining *punyabhumi*. His definition of Hindu – unlike Hindutva – was narrow, put Christians and Muslims beyond the purview of nationhood and was consistent with a belief that re-conversions to the Hindu fold were the only way to arrest this change of nationality. What emerges from this very brief overview is the amazing extent to which Savarkar has influenced contemporary Hindu nationalism, both in its positive and negative facets.[13]

Dasgupta was wrong in holding that the RSS' concept of 'cultural nationalism' was different from Savarkar's Hindutva. The BJP itself regards them as being synonymous. He, however pointed out that 'Savarkar's limited view of *punyabhumi* has tacitly given legitimacy to vicious anti-Muslim tendencies which have also manifested themselves after December 6.'

Dasgupta pines for an 'enlightened Hindutva' minus the hate. In thus trying to square the circle he is not alone. Vajpayee also tried it in a pathetic venture. On March 27, 2002, he said, 'when Swami Vivekananda speaks of Hindutva, nobody can call him a communalist'. But some 'defined Hindutva in such a manner that it is better to keep a distance from it.'[14] And again, on May 6, he said: 'I accept the Hindutva of Swami Vivekananda. But the kind of Hindutva being propagated now is wrong and one should be wary of it.'[15]

The truth, as Vajpayee is doubtless aware, is that Swami Vivekananda did not speak of Hindutva at all. He was concerned with the profundities of Hinduism. It was Savarkar who 'coined' the term Hindutva in 1923 to propagate a cult of hate.

The noted historian Tapan Raychaudhuri says of Vivekananda that 'he was among the earliest nationalist thinkers to claim the Indo-Islamic past as part of the Indian heritage'. He noted with disgust that, 'the VHP has the audacity to claim him as their own'. 'It is difficult', he argued, 'to imagine him [Vivekananda] as the ideological ancestor of people who incite the ignorant to destroy other people's places of worship in a revanchist spirit.'[16] The intellectual progenitor of the Hindutva project is not Vivekananda, but Savarkar. Andersen and Damle note that 'a major influence on his [the RSS founder Hedgewar's] thinking was a handwritten manuscript of . . . Savarkar's *Hindutva* which advanced the thesis that the Hindus were a nation'.[17] And Keer records that 'one of the early visitors to Savarkar in Ratnagiri was the great founder of the RSS, Dr K.B. Hedgewar. The interview took place in 1925 at Shirgaon, a village on the outskirts of Ratnagiri.' *Hindutva* had just been published. 'Before starting' the RSS, Hedgewar 'had a long discussion with Savarkar over the faith, form and future of the organization.'[18]

### The origins of the term

We must consult Savarkar's book for a proper understanding of his thinking. It explains why it had the impact it did. *Hindutva provides a coherent self-contained ideology of hate. Its assertiveness stills doubt and provides assurance.*

The publisher of the essay, S.S. Savarkar, revealed in his Preface to the Second Edition that 'it was during his stay from 1906 to 1910 in England that the attention of Veer Savarkarji was drawn pointedly to the question as to who can be precisely called a "Hindu"' (p. i). Young as he was then, Savarkar was at the crossroads of Indian nationalism and Hindu communalism. He did his initial writing in the Andamans. It was put into final shape in Ratnagiri Jail and smuggled out. The first edition was published under the pseudonym, 'A Maratha', by V.V. Kelkar, a Nagpur lawyer. We are told that Lala Lajpat Rai, Pandit Madan Mohan Malaviya and several others hailed it 'as the most *original* and scholarly contribution to the Hindu ideology' (p. vii).

S.S. Savarkar, publisher of the second edition, emphasized that the author, V.D. Savarkar,

> had to *coin* some new words such as 'Hindutva', 'Hinduness', 'Hindudom' in order to express [the] totality of the cultural, historical, and above all the national aspects along with the religious one, which mark out the Hindu people as a whole. The definition is not consequently meant to be a definition of Hindu-Dharma, or Hindu religion. It is a definition of 'Hindutva', 'Hinduness'. It is essentially national in its outlook and comprehends the Hindu People as a Hindu-Rashtra.' Hindutva is a new term for a new ideology, the ideology of 'Hindu-Rashtra' (a Hindu State). (p. iv)

The author endorsed the publisher's understanding in the section entitled 'Hindutva is different from Hinduism'. Savarkar wrote,

> *Here it is enough to point out that Hindutva is not identical with*

> *what is vaguely indicated by the term Hinduism.* By an 'ism' it is generally meant a theory or a code more or less based on spiritual or religious dogma or system. But when we attempt to investigate into the essential significance of Hindutva we do not primarily – and certainly not mainly – concern ourselves with any particular theocratic or religious dogma or creed. Had not linguistic usage stood in our way then 'Hinduness' would have certainly been a better word than Hinduism as a near parallel to Hindutva. (p. 4)

### The two-nation theory

The section 'Hindus, a nation' makes Savarkar the first to propound the two-nation theory in 1923. Consider this passage, full of hatred and venom:

> Everything that is common in us with our enemies, weakens our power of opposing them. The foe that has nothing in common with us is the foe likely to be most bitterly resisted by us just as a friend that has almost everything in him that we admire and prize in ourselves is likely to be the friend we love most. *The necessity of creating a bitter sense of wrong and invoking a power of undying resistance especially in India that had under the opiates of Universalism and non-violence lost the faculty even of resisting sin and crime and aggression, could best be accomplished by cutting off even the semblance of a common worship* – a common Church which required her to clasp the hand of those as her coreligionists whose had been the very hand that had strangled her as a nation.

The identity of his 'foes' is obvious.

Savarkar's persistent reference to 'Sindhasthan' and 'Sindhu' (pp. 30–31) explain Advani's recently acquired passion for the Indus and with it pleas for undoing the partition of India as urged by Savarkar.[19] To proceed with Savarkar's *Hindutva*, the author traced 'chapters of the history of the words Hindu and Hindusthan from the earliest Vedic period to the fall of the last of our Hindu empire in 1818 A.D. . . . We are now in a position to address ourselves to the main task of determining the essentials of Hindutva' (p. 70). To begin with, 'territorial nationalism' is totally rejected, 'although the root-meaning of the word Hindu like the sister epithet Hindi may mean only an Indian, yet as it is we would be straining the usage of words too much – we fear, to the point of breaking – if we call a Mohammedan a Hindu because of his being a resident of India' (p. 83). Further,

> An American may become a citizen of India. He would certainly be entitled, if bona fide, to be treated as our Bharatiya or Hindi, a countryman and a fellow citizen of ours. But as long as in addition to our country, he has not adopted our culture and our history, inherited our blood and has come to look upon our land not only as the land of his love *but even of his worship*, he cannot get himself incorporated into the Hindu fold. For although the first requisite of Hindutva is that he be a citizen of Hindusthan either by himself or through his forefathers, yet it is not the only requisite qualification of it, as the term Hindu has come to mean much more than its geographical significance.
>
> The reason that explains why the term Hindu cannot be synonymous with Bharatiya or Hindi and mean an Indian only, naturally introduces us to the second essential implication of that term. The Hindus are not merely the citizens of the Indian state because they are united not only by the bonds of the love they bear to a common motherland but also by the bonds of a common blood. (p. 84)

Having discarded 'territorial nationalism', he moves to 'cultural nationalism'.

> We Hindus are bound together not only by the tie of the love we bear to a common fatherland and by the common blood that courses through our veins and keeps our hearts

> throbbing and our affections warm, but also by the tie of the common homage we pay to our great civilization – *our Hindu culture*, which could not be better rendered than by the word Sanskriti suggestive as it is of that language, Sanskrit, which has been the chosen means of expression and preservation of that culture, of all that was best and worth-preserving in the history of our race. We are one because we are a nation a race and own a common Sanskriti (civilization). (pp. 91–32)

Thus the BJP is absolutely correct in arguing that 'Hindutva' and 'cultural nationalism' are synonymous.

### Fatherland and holyland

Savarkar alleges that Muslims and Christians 'belong, or feel that they belong to a cultural unit altogether different from the Hindu one' (p. 101). The crucial test, then, is two-fold. *Pitribhumi* (Fatherland) must be the same as *Punyabhumi* (Holyland):

> To every Hindu, from the Santal to the Sadhu this Bharata bhumi this Sindhusthan is at once a Pitribhu and a Punyabhu-fatherland and a holy land.
>
> That is why in the case of some of our Mohammedan or Christian countrymen who had originally been forcibly converted to a non-Hindu religion and who consequently have inherited along with Hindus, a common Fatherland and a greater part of the wealth of a common culture – language, law, customs, folklore and history – are not and cannot be recognized as Hindus. For though Hindusthan to them is Fatherland as to any other Hindu yet it is not to them a Holy land too. Their holy land is far off in Arabia or Palestine. Their mythology and Godmen, ideas and heroes are not the children of this soil. Consequently their names and their outlook smack of a foreign origin. (p. 113)

If Muslims and Christians accept the Hindu faith they become Hindus.

> Ye, who by race, by blood, by culture, by nationality possess almost all the essentials of Hindutva and had been forcibly snatched out of our ancestral home by the hand of violence – ye, have only to render wholehearted love to our common Mother and recognize her not only as Fatherland (Pitribhu) but even as a Holyland (Punyabhu), and ye would be most welcome to the Hindu fold.
>
> This is a choice which our countrymen and our old kith and kin, the Bohras, Khojas, Memons and other Mohammedan and Christian communities are free to make – a choice again which must be a choice of love. But as long as they are not minded thus, so long they cannot be recognized as Hindus.
>
> These are the essentials of Hindutva – a common nation (Rashtra) a common race (Jati) and a common civilization (Sanskriti). All these essentials could best be summed up by stating in brief that he is a Hindu to whom Sindhusthan is not only a Pitribhu but also a Punyabhu. For the first two essentials of Hindutva – nation and Jati – are clearly denoted and connoted by the word Pitrubhu while the third essential of Sanskriti is pre-eminently implied by the word Punyabhu, as it is precisely Sanskriti including Sanskaras i.e. rites and rituals, ceremonies and sacraments, that makes a land a Holyland. (p. 116)

For the minorities, then, the option of retaining both their faith *and* their Indian nationality is extinguished. This is the reality of the Hindu *rashtra* based on Hindutva.

This is not a restatement of the ancient philosophy and faith of Hinduism. It is the formulation of a new political ideology of hate – Hindutva. More than anyone else, Savarkar himself is aware of the novelty of his ideological enterprise. Therefore, towards the end of his essay, he repeats what he had said at the outset – a *new* word, Hindutva, was being '*coined*'.

> There would have been no serious objection raised against the *cultural aspect of Hindutva* too, but for the unfortunate misunderstanding that owes its origin to the confusing similarity between the two terms, Hindutva and Hinduism. *We have tried already to draw a clear line of demarcation between the two conceptions* and protected against the wrong use of the word Hinduism to denote the Sanatan Dharma alone. *Hindutva is not identical with Hindu Dharma,* nor is Hindu Dharma identical with Hindusim. (p. 121)

## The Hindutva judgement

If an undergraduate writing an essay on Hindutva were to ignore the mass of material on the subject and pronounce that 'ordinarily Hindutva is understood as a way of life or a state of mind and it is not to be equated with or understood as religious Hindu fundamentalism', he would receive a deserved and stinging rebuke. But the words quoted here were used by Justice J.S. Verma of the Supreme Court in a shocking judgement which held that neither the Shiv Sena chief Bal Thackeray nor his colleague Manohar Joshi violated Section 123(3) of the Representation of the People Act, 1951, which penalizes appeals to the voter 'on the ground of religion.'[20] Shockingly Justice Verma's judgement on Hindutva ignored Savarkar's work on the subject. The judge equated Hindutva with Hinduism in a laboured effort. Millions of devout Hindus despise Hindutva. Justice Verma is, of course, entitled to differ with them. He has no right, however, to equate Hindutva with Hinduism in a judicial pronouncement. That he went so far as to rule that 'the word "Hindutva" is used and understood as a synonym of "Indianization"' – the Jan Sangh's slogan – reveals his outlook, especially since these remarks were *obiter* and unnecessary for deciding the case. Justice Verma had studiously refrained from pronouncing secularism to be a 'basic feature' of the Constitution in the S.R. Bommai case (1994) SCC. His judgement in the Ayodhya case was just as flawed.[21]

The BJP, understandingly, lauds his rulings as judicial exoneration of its ideology of state. Few know that the court as a whole did not share Justice Verma's view. The matter was referred to a larger bench. It is unfortunate that the court has not found time to hear that reference. Justice Verma's ruling is productive of grave public mischief and deserves to be reviewed and rejected.

The BJP's 1999 Manifesto dishonestly claimed that 'the Supreme Court, too, finally, endorsed the true meaning and content of Hindutva as being consistent with the true meaning and definition of secularism.' This is utterly false. *The Court's final ruling is yet to be given* and the BJP knows this very well, like every one else. On April 16, 1996 a three-member Bench of the Court, comprising Justices K. Ramaswamy, S.P. Bharucha and K.S. Paripoornan referred to a larger Bench of five judges the highly unsatisfactory judgement given by Justice J.S. Verma, on December 11, 1995, on behalf of himself and Justices N.P. Singh and K. Venkataswami.[22] It is, therefore, not a final ruling on Hindutva.[23]

The background is important. In an earlier case decided on July 14, 1995, by Justices G.N. Ray and Faizan Uddin, the Supreme Court clearly said:

> It has been very strenuously contended by the learned council for the appellant that appeal to vote for 'Hindutva' should not be confused with appeal to vote only for a member of one community namely the Hindus. Criticism of partisan treatment meted out to the Hindus by the ruling Congress party or appeasement policy in favour of one community or followers of a particular religion impairing national integrity and appeal to oppose such improper and anti-national policy should not be held to be an appeal to vote only on the basis of a particular religion. It has been contended that the thrust of the speeches was that unequal treatment meted out to Hindus and deliberate hurting of sentiments of Hindus have encouraged divisive forces and anti-national elements in the country and Hindus should be aware of such divisive and anti-national forces in selecting proper candidate who would safeguard the unity and integrity of the country. Hindus should be aware of such divisive forces and try to unite against such divisive and anti-

> national forces in selecting proper candidate who would safeguard the unity and integrity of the country. In our view, it is not necessary to consider the philosophy of Hindu religion and its tenets of tolerance and respect for different religious faiths for the purpose of appreciating whether appeal was really made for Hindutva which is something different from outward practices and some of the following professed by followers of Hindu religion. In the instant case, we have already indicated that the appellant had given publicity to the voters by exhibiting the poster Ext. 0-20 which was *per se* highly offensive and potentially vulnerable and was likely to bring hatred and misunderstanding between the two communities, namely, the Hindus and the Muslims. In our view, the poster containing an appeal to vote for the appellant 'to teach the Muslims a lesson' cannot be justified in any manner even by giving reasonable latitudes in election speeches.[24]

The Appellant's election was set aside because of that poster.

That bench adopted an approach wholly opposite to the one over which Justce Verma presided. He did not refer to this earlier case. Worse, he distorted a quote, omitting what totally refuted his thesis. The Supreme Court itself has ruled time and again that a precedent must be read in the context of the facts of that particular case. Hinduism may be hard to define. Not so Hindutva. Unless, of course, one deliberately identifies it with Hinduism. Justice Verma did just that: 'Ordinarily, Hindutva is understood as a way of life or a state of mind and it is not to be equated with or understood as religious Hindu fundamentalism'.

Did Justice Verma cite any authority in support of this weird conclusion? Yes, he did. The quotation and his inference deserve to be set out in full.

> In *Indian Muslims – the Need for a Positive Outlook* by Maulana Wahiduddin Khan (1994), it is said: 'The strategy worked out to solve the minorities problem was, although differently worded, that of Hindutva or Indianization. This strategy,

> briefly stated, aims at developing a uniform culture by obliterating the differences between all of the cultures co-existing in the country. This was felt to be the way to communal harmony and national unity. It was thought that this would put an end once and for all to the minorities problem.'

From this Justice Verma concluded, 'The above opinion indicates that the word "Hindutva" is used and understood as a synonym of "Indianization", i.e. development of uniform culture by obliterating the difference between all the cultures co-existing in the country.' Where was the need to pick on this one obscure book? The Maulana is a polemicist. There are works by academics which are truly authoritative. In a judgement of this kind, surely such works ought to be quoted.

However, even if the Maulana is to be quoted, surely he must be quoted fairly and understood properly. If one does that, one finds that far from supporting Justice Verma's conclusion, the Maulana refutes it thoroughly. *It was not in praise of Hindutva* or its euphemism 'Indianization' that the Maulana was writing, *but in their censure.* The paragraph preceding it lamented that Hindus did not treat the Partition as 'just an incident in past history'. The subsequent strategy 'to solve the minorities problem' through Hindutva or Indianization, sought to *impose* 'a uniform culture by obliterating the differences between all of the cultures co-existing in the country'. Unlike Justice Verma who quoted this to imply approval of this process, the Maulana *disapproved* of it. He is for the co-existence of 'all of the cultures' in our diverse land. The BJP and the RSS are not. This becomes all too clear from the very sentence after the Maulana's comment that it was thought that the obliteration would end the minorities problem. That sentence reads: 'However beautiful this suggestion may appear to be, *it is certainly impracticable*'. Justice Verma did not note this sentence at all.

As for 'Indianization', the Standing Committee of the NIC adopted a statement, on October 16, 1969, which said: 'We condemn the spread of the idea that any community requires to be Indianized.' An all-party conference was convened under its auspices on

November 3, 1969, with the Prime Minister, Indira Gandhi, in the chair. It denounced Indianization. The Jan Sangh alone opted out. Indianization was a subterfuge for Hindutva.[25]

The reference to the larger bench, it must be noted, is not confined to the narrow issue of a candidate's responsibility for the speeches of his party leaders. 'The content and scope' of the relevant provision of Section 123 (3) and 3A of the Representation of the People Act, 1951 (penalizing communal propaganda) are also referred to the larger Bench 'lest miscarriage of justice in interpretation of "corrupt practice" . . . would ensue' (p. 671, para 12). This Bench's disquiet at Justice Verma's ruling is manifest.

### On to Golwalkar

To Savarkar, the author of Hindutva, tolerance of diversity among Indians is unthinkable:

> Let our minorities remember that if strength lies in union, then in Hindutva lies the firmest and yet the dearest bond that can effect a real, lasting and powerful union of our people. You may fancy that it pays you to remain aloof for the passing hour, but it would do incalculable harm to this our ancient race and civilization as a whole – and especially to yourselves.

Now, consider this:

> Today we often hear our political leaders speaking of 'national integration' and so on. But what is that 'common emotion', that common basis on which all can come together? What are those eternal life-springs of our national life that go to make it unified, resurgent and glorious? In the first place, the feeling of burning devotion to the land, which from times immemorial we have regarded as our sacred Matrubhoomi, – in the second place, the feeling of fellowship, of fraternity, born out of the realization that we are the children of that one great common Mother, – in

> the third place, the intense awareness of a common current of national life, born out of a common culture and heritage, of common history and traditions, of common ideals and aspirations, – this trinity of values or, in a word, Hindu Nationalism, forms the bedrock of our national edifice.[26]

These words are *not* by Savarkar. They have been written by M.S. Golwalkar. Their views are strikingly identical. Every nuance in Savarkar's *Hindutva* is present in Golwalkar's *Thoughts.* What comes through most of all is the hate and damnation of others at their very birth. Sample this:

> Some wise men of today tell us that no man is born as Hindu or Muslim or Christian but as a simple human being. This may be true about others. But for a Hindu, he gets the first samskar when he is still in the mother's womb, and the last when his body is consigned to the flames. There are sixteen samskars for the Hindu, which make him what he is. In fact, we are Hindus even before we emerge from the womb of our mother. We are therefore born as Hindus. About the others, they are born to this world as simple unnamed human beings and later on, either circumcised or baptized, they become Muslims or Christians. (p. 118)

Golwalkar devotes an entire chapter to denouncing 'Territorial Nationalism' (chapter X, pp. 136–57). He held that

> here was already a full-fledged ancient nation of the Hindus and the various communities which were living in the country were here either as guests, the Jews and Parsis, or as invaders, the Muslims and Christians. They never faced the question how all such heterogeneous groups could be called as children of the soil merely because, *by an accident, they happened to reside in a common territory under the rule of a common enemy.* . . . The theories of territorial nationalism and of common danger, which formed the basis for our concept of nation, had deprived us of the positive and inspiring

> content of our real Hindu Nationhood and made many of the freedom movements virtually anti British movements. *Anti-Britishism was equated with patriotism and nationalism.* This reactionary view has had disastrous effects upon the entire course of the freedom struggle, its leaders and the common people. (p. 142)

Golwalkar's denunciation of Gandhi was as coarse as Savarkar's:

> Here we had leaders who were, as if, pledged to sap all manliness from their own people. However, this is not a mere accident of history. This leadership only came as a bitter climax of the despicable tribe of so many of our ancestors who during the past twelve hundred years sold their national honour and freedom to foreigners, and joined hands with the inveterate enemies of our country and our religion in cutting the throats of their own kith and kin to gratify their personal egoism, selfishness and rivalry. *No wonder nemesis overtook such a people in the form of such a self-destruction.* (p. 153)

Gowalkar clarified,

> today, there is a misconception even regarding the word 'Bhartiya'. It is commonly used as a translation of the word 'Indian' which includes all the various communities like the Muslim, Christian, Parsi, etc. residing in this land. So, the word 'Bhartiya' too is likely to mislead us when we want to denote our particular society. The word 'Hindu' alone connotes correctly and completely the meaning what we want to convey.' (p. 98)

Like Savarkar, Golwalkar concluded, 'All the requisites for making a full fledged nation are thus fulfilled in the life of this great Hindu People. Therefore, we say that in this land of ours, Bharat, *the national life is of the Hindu People.* In short, *this is the Hindu*

*Nation*' (p. 126). Gowalkar also endorses the dual test of holyland and fatherland. 'They (Muslims and Christians) look to some foreign lands as their holy places' (p. 128).

Gowalkar exhorts,

> if we are to rise again as a nation, we must correct the initial blunder which we committed in accepting a new fangled idea of nationalism, which experience has proved to be absolutely false and ruinous. Let us not be deluded into a wrong track by the wily propaganda of interested persons. We have been sufficiently fooled up till now by their exhortation that we Hindus, who are having a great philosophy of human brotherhood, catholicity of spirit and so on, should not narrow ourselves by the talk of Hindu Nationalism and all such 'communal', 'medieval', and 'reactionary' ideas. We must be able to see through the game and revert to the truth of our nationalism as an ancient fact and the Hindus being the national society of Bharat, as so clearly restated by our revered founder when we decided the word 'Rashtriya' for our organization [Rashtriya Swayamsevak Sangh, RSS]. (pp. 156-57)

This is the man whom Advani, Vajpayee and company for long hailed as 'Guruji' (mentor). Not one BJP leader has yet criticized Gowalkar for his venous expression of hatred for Muslims.

> History has recorded that their antagonism was not merely political. Had it been so, they could have been won over in a very short time. But it was so deep-rooted that whatever we believed in, the Muslim was wholly hostile to it. If we worship in the temple, he would desecrate it. If we carry on bhajans and car [sic] festivals, that would irritate him. If we worship cow, he would like to eat it. If we glorify women as a symbol of sacred motherhood, he would like to molest her. He was tooth and nail opposed to our way of life in all aspects – religious, cultural, social etc. He had imbibed that hostility to the very core. (p. 148)

Now, consider what the BJP proposes in its election manifestos:

> With a BJP Government at the Centre, the next five years will be devoted to implementing our Manifesto based on the four concepts of *Suraksha, Shuchita, Swadeshi* and *Samrasata. Hindutva, or cultural nationalism,* shall be the rainbow which will bridge our present to our glorious past and pave the way for an equally glorious future; it will guide the transition from *swarajya* to *surajya.*
>
> Our nationalist vision is not merely bound by the geographical or political identity of Bharat but it is referred by our timeless cultural heritage, this cultural heritage which is central to all regions, religions and languages, is a civilizational identity and constitutes the cultural nationalism of India which is the core of Hindutva. This we believe is the identity of our ancient nation 'Bharatvarsha'. . . . The BJP is convinced that Hindutva has immense potentiality to re-energize this nation and strengthen and discipline it to undertake the arduous task of nation-building. This can and does trigger a higher level of patriotism that can transform the country to greater levels of efficiency and performance. It is with such integrative ideas in mind, the BJP joined the Ram Janmabhoomi movement for the construction of Shri Ram Mandir at Ayodhya. This greatest mass movement in post-Independence history reoriented the disoriented polity in India and strengthened the foundation of *cultural nationalism.*

An unbroken ideological thread binds Savarkar, Golwalkar, and the BJP. This writer has advisedly refrained from quoting at any length Savarkar's comments on Muslims. He was, if anything, even more coarse than Gowalkar, which is saying a lot. There is no form of vice or depravity which Savarkar did not ascribe to Muslims, especially in *Six Epochs of Hindu History.* The BJP invites the nation – in which, presumably, Muslims and Christians are included – to regard *this* man as a 'national hero'.

## The Hindu Mahasabha

The Hindu Mahasabha was founded on April 9, 1915 at Hardwar. 'In its earlier phase . . . it functioned as a socio-religious organization designed to check the downward filtration of Western liberal influences in the Hindu Society, especially when these operated through the agency of the Government'. But politics was not absent. Its first President Maharaja Manindra Chandra Nandy 'expressed a fear that Hindus might be reduced even to a minority' in India.[27]

Revived at Varanasi in August 1923 by Madan Mohan Malaviya, the Mahasabha emerged as an important player in Indian politics. Lala Lajpat Rai was President at its eighth session in 1925.[28] The founder of the RSS, Dr Hedgewar, maintained close links with it and with Savarkar. Many were members of both the Mahasabha and the RSS. Disputes broke out after a number of members of the RSS left it in order to escape its constraints on political activity. Prominent among them was Nathuram Godse who formed the para-military Hindu Rashtra Dal.[29] As we shall see, Godse's loyalty to the RSS remained undiminished till the end. The differences were only on the question of tactics.

With Savarkar's election as President of the Hindu Mahasabha in 1937, after his release that year, the party became even more militant and rabid. We have in *Hindu Rashtra Darshan* a collection of his presidential speeches from 1937 to 1942. He was even more forthright in his advocacy of Hindutva now than in his book of 1923 and amplified the nuances in the concept.[30] Indeed, Savarkar spoke as if he was picking up the ideas from his book and elaborating on them:

> a definition must in the main respond to reality. Just as by the first constituent of Hindutva, the possession of a common Holyland – the Indian Mahommedans, Jews, Christians, Parsees, etc. are excluded from claiming themselves as Hindus which in reality also they do not, – in spite of their recognizing Hindustan as their fatherland, so also on the other hand the second constituent of the definition, that of possessing a common fatherland excludes

> the Japanese, the Chinese and others from the Hindu fold in spite of the fact of their having a Holyland in common with us. (p. 6)

As always, he was at pains to clarify that Hindutva was an altogether new concept:

> the concept of the term 'Hindutva' – Hinduness – is more comprehensive than the word 'Hinduism'. It was to draw a pointed attention to this distinction that I had coined the words 'Hindutva', 'Pan Hindu' and 'Hindudom' when I framed the definition of the word 'Hindu', Hinduism concerns with the religious systems of the Hindus, their theology or dogma. But this is precisely a matter, which this Hindu Mahasabha leaves entirely to individual or group conscience and faith. The Mahasabha takes its stand on no dogma, no book or school of philosophy whether pantheist, monotheist or atheist. . . .
>
> The Mahasabha is not in the main a Hindu-Dharma-Sabha but it is pre-eminently a Hindu-Rashtra-Sabha and is a Pan-Hindu organization shaping the destiny of the Hindu Nation in all its social, political and cultural aspects. Those who commit the serious mistake of taking the Hindu Mahasabha for only a religious body would do well to keep this distinction in mind. (pp. 8–9)

In 1937 he declared, 'So far as the Hindus are concerned there can be no distinction nor conflict in the least between our Communal and National duties, as the best interests of the Hindudom are simply identified with best interests of Hindusthan as a whole' (p. 1) Half a century later, Vajpayee echoed this theme. He said, on September 24, 1989 at the BJP's National Executive, that Hindu sentiments were synonymous with the national interest.[31]

Savarkar launched a major political offensive in good Göbbelsian style.

> I warn the Hindus that the Mohammedans are likely to prove

> dangerous to our Hindu Nation and the existence of a common Indian State even if and when England goes out. Let us not be stone blind to the fact that they as a community still continue to cherish fanatical designs to establish a Moslem rule in India. . . . We Hindus must have a country of our own in the Solar System and must continue to flourish there as Hindus – descendants of a mighty people. Then up with the *Shuddi* which has not a religious meaning alone *but a political side as well.* Up with Sanghatan for the consummation of which it is simply imperative for Hindus to *capture whatever political power has been wrung out by our efforts in the past under the present Reforms Act.* (p. 27)

### The Mahasabha and the British

Unlike the Congress, Savarkar was only too willing to accept whatever crumbs of power the British offered Indians. On this point, this 'revolutionary' and 'freedom fighter' was constant, from 1917 to 1937. He reiterated this theme in 1938 also. 'If but the Hindu Sanghatanists capture the seats that are allotted to the Hindus under the present constitution in Municipalities, Boards and Legislatures you will find that a sudden lift is given to the Hindu movement so as to raise it to an incredible power in relation to your present all-round helplessness' (p. 71)

That is why Savarkar's staunch supporter, Shyama Prasad Mookerjee, joined Fazlul Haq's Ministry in Bengal, and Hindu Mahasabhites joined the Muslim League Ministries in Sind. The Congress historian Pattabhi Sitaramayya recorded: 'It is noteworthy that the Hindu [Maha] Sabha ministers of Sind remained passive spectators to the passing of a resolution in favour of Pakistan by the Sind Legislature and contended themselves with a protest that remained . . . unimpressive.'[32] They did not resign their offices.

Mookerjee not only professed 'loyalty to my leader' (Fazlul Haq) but, in a long letter, advised the Governor of Bengal, Sir John Herbert, how to crush the 'Quit India' movement. As if the Governor required such encouragement from any one! Mookerjee wrote:

> It is of utmost importance that *there should be complete understanding between you, as Governor, and your colleagues during the present critical period.* . . . Let me now refer to the situation that may be created in the province as a result of any *widespread movement launched by the Congress.* Anybody, who during the war, plans to stir up mass feelings, resulting in internal disturbances or insecurity, *must be resisted by any Government* that may function for the time being. But mere repression is no remedy when the promoters of the movement assert and make people believe that they too want to resist the impending attacks of the enemy, not as a slave country but as a free one, but the Ruling Authority is determined not to transfer real power to the children of the soil. . . .
>
> As regards India's attitude towards England, *the struggle between them, if any, should not take place at this juncture.* The present war is being fought not for perpetuation of British domination over India. Old ideas of Imperialism must be buried underground, and they are not going to revive, whatever the result of the present war may be. . . .
>
> But many of your permanent officers, and I believe you also, influenced as you are by their opinion, very often tremble at the thought of accepting the co-operation of patriotic Bengalis who, to put it even at its worst, were hitherto the enemies of British policy in India. Here you have to rise to the full height of your statesmanship if you can hope to discharge truly the great responsibility of your office. If I were to deal with them in my own way, I would immediately establish personal contact with all of them and offer them a willing hand of co-operation.[33]

Quite clearly, Mookerjee was making an offer to help the British crush the Congress and the Quit India movement. Had the British agreed, Mookherjee would have enthusiastically served as their hatchetman. It was to be a Mahasabha-British pact against the Congress on the lines his leader had offered the Viceroy in *Mumbai* on October 9, 1939. Mookerjee left no room for doubt on this score.

> The question is *how to combat this movement in Bengal?* The administration of the province should be carried on in such a manner that in spite of the best efforts of the Congress, this movement will fail to take root in the province. It should be possible for us, specially responsible ministers, to be able to tell the public that the freedom for which the Congress has started the movement, already belongs to the representatives of the people.[34]

The British knew that it was the Congress, not the Mahasabha, which mattered. Mookerjee's offer was spurned. Sensing his isolation, he resigned on November 16, 1942. But, while doing so, raised issues he had not in his offer.

An entry of January 6, 1946 in his diary provides a clue to his heir, the BJP's, policies. 'As seventy-five percent of the population were Hindus, and if India was to adopt a democratic form of government, the Hindus would automatically play a major role in it'.[35] Gandhi and Nehru rejected this view consistently. True enough that Hindus constitute a majority in India while the rest comprise the minorities. But it is a *political,* not a *communal* majority, that would rule India as Indians sharing power with fellow Indians.

Archival researches by the distinguished scholar Joya Chatterji reveal that, besides endorsing Savarkar's two-nation theory, Mookerjee also shared Savarkar's hatred for Muslims. 'For many bhadralok Hindus [including Mookerjee], the sense of superiority in relation to Muslims was fed by the belief that Bengali Muslims were, by and large, "a set of converts" from the dregs of the Hindu society.'[36] To Savarkar, Gowalkar and Mookerjee, Hindus and Muslims, as members of two nations, were not only different but the Muslims belonged to an *inferior* breed of humans. The perversity in their reasoning is breathtaking. Consider how Savarkar looks at the formation of the Indian National Congress and the beginning of the nationalist movement in India:

> If India, because it was a territorial unit and called a country

> must be a national unit as well, then all of us must also be Indians only and cease to be Hindus or Moslems, Christians or Parsees. So they, the leaders of those first generations of English educated people, being almost all Hindus, tried their best to cease themselves to be Hindus and thought it below their dignity to take any cognizance of the divisions as Hindus and Moslems and became transformed overnight into Indian patriots alone. . . . It is to be noted that the British Government favoured the movement and it was a Viceroy who sponsored it. Many a prominent British civilian like Mr. Hume, Wedderburn and others led it for a long time. Great Hindu leaders from the most public-spirited motives nursed it and it became the organized and authoritative spokesman of the new cult of Indian Patriotism. (*HRD*, pp. 48–49)

Ergo, the Congress was a British creation. He exhorted Hindus to retreat from the high road of Indian nationalism and enter, instead, the dark alley of communalism.

> Let us Hindu Sanghathnists first correct the original mistake, the original political sin which our Hindu Congressites most unwillingly committed at the beginning of the Indian National Congress movement and are persistently committing still of running after *the mirage of a territorial Indian Nation* and of seeking to kill as an impediment in that fruitless pursuit the life growth of an organic Hindu Nation. (p. 63)

This is the Savarkar whom his hitherto closet devotees Advani and Vajpayee have began to applaud publicly.

Consistently enough, Savarkar asked that the tricolour be rejected as a national flag. 'Gerva [saffron] Flag shall be the Flag of the Hindu Nation. With its OM, the Swastik and the Sword, it appeals to the sentiments cherished by our race ever since the Vaidik days' (p. 106).

Peddling lies and rumours is an old communalist trick. This, too, has a long history, and can be traced back to Savarkar. On several occasions, Savarkar attributed to Gandhi or Nehru propositions they had never advanced. As examples, we quote below four such statements, each one of them an outright lie.

> Pandit Nehru thinks, leaving even Maulana Abul Kalam Azad far behind who only proposes Hindusthani which he assures us is tantamount to Urdu, that the highly Arabianized Urdu of the Aligarh School or the Osmania University School is best fitted to be the National Language of India including of course some twenty-eight crores of Hindus. (p. 110)

> In demanding three votes for one Moslem, the Moslem League is outrageously communal, while in calling upon the Hindus to yield to this demand and accede to the proposal of one vote for three Hindus, the Congress is cowardly communal! (p. 121)

> What is most surprising to note is the fact that these Hindu leaders outbid even the Ali Brothers, the 'National' Maulana Azad and other Moslem leaders in maintaining that if the Amir succeed in capturing Delhi, we would have won Swaraj! – for they definitely stated that the rule of the Afghans was in itself Swaraj. (p. 127)

> During the [First World War] the Ex-Amir Amanulla Khan was to play the part of the destined deliverer of Islam in India and with the treacherous connivance of Gandhiji, the two great 'Nationalists' leaders, the Ali Brothers, conspired to bring him to Delhi as the would-be anointed Emperor of India. (p. 237)

### Links with Nazis

Recent scholarship has brought to light the fact that the RSS-Mahasabha leadership not only held Hitler and Mussolini in great admiration, but that there were more concrete links between these fascists across continents. Marzia Casolari has meticulously documented Savarkar as well as Gowalkar's enchantment with Nazi Germany.[37]

Savarkar supported Hitler's annexation of the Sudeten parts of Czechoslovakia and his annexation of Austria. Golwalkar, another racial purist, admired Hitler's brutal purge of the Jews (pp. 223–24). But in the course of her archival research Marzia Casolari not only found evidence of 'direct contacts between the representatives of the fascist regime, including Mussolini and Hindu nationalists,' but evidence also of a far closer relationship between the RSS and the Hindu Mahasabha than the former would care to acknowledge today. *This bears on the relationship between Savarkar and Godse, on the one hand, and, on the other between, the RSS and Godse.* We shall come to that in some detail in the following chapter.

Marzia Casolari has put the record straight on the Mahasabha-RSS relationship:

> According to the commonly accepted opinion – *supported by the organizations of militant Hinduism* – the RSS and the Hindu Mahasabha have never been particularly close, and, during Savarkar's presidentship, they severed their links. *Reality, however, seems to be different.* In fact, the available documentation shows not only that such a split never happened, but that the two organizations always had close connections. We should not forget that Hedgewar had been secretary to the Hindu Mahasabha from 1926 to 1931 [note 13 of Casolari's text]. The RSS seems to have provided support to the Hindu Mahasabha, as shown by the fact that groups of RSS militants used to gather at the public meetings organized to celebrate Savarkar's release [note 14 of Casolari's text].[38]

Footnotes 13 and 14 bear reproduction *in extensor*:

> 13. It seems, moreover, that Hedgewar was deeply influenced by the ideas expressed in Savarkar's *Hindutva*. When

Hedgewar decided to found his organization, he went to Ratnagiri to meet Savarkar, in order to obtain from him suggestions and advice. Subsequently, during Savarkar's internment in Ratnagiri, Hedgewar had continuously been in touch with Babarao Savarkar. Among Hedgewar papers, in Nagpur, I found several letters exchanged between Hedgewar and Babarao Savarkar, who was closely connected to the RSS.

14. On several occasions, after having been released, Savarkar congratulated 'the Rashtriya Swayam Sewak Sangh of Dr. Hedgewar of Nagpur on its work and discipline'. At the 'guru purnima' celebrated by the RSS on July 29, 1939, Savarkar gave a speech to approximately 5,000 people, while several years later, during the RSS officers' training camp OTC, which took place in Pune during May 27 to 29, 1943, in the presence of Golwalkar, Babarao Savarkar, B.S. Moonje and about 5,000 people, the former president of the Hindu Mahasabha expressed his pleasure to see the display by Swayamsewaks in great number and said that he was proud to see the Hindu youths, boys and girls, joining the institutions, based on Hinduism, in great number. Militants had also the habit of collecting donations for their leader. In August 1937 in Pune, the local Hindu militants and sympathizers offered him Rs 250. Several years later, on the occasion of Savarkar's 61$^{st}$ birthday, considerable donations were collected by the exponents of the Hindu organizations Savarkar visited during one of his propaganda tours. At the above-mentioned OTC camp, where Savarkar celebrated his birthday, Rs 1,80,000 had been collected by Hindu organizations, Pune municipality, and private citizens, respectively.[39]

### RSS and Mahasabha: friends or foes?

Other archival discoveries fortify Marzia Casolari's findings, most notably in one of the volumes of the *Towards Freedom* series.[40] That explains why the Government of India prevented publication of other volumes in the series by Profs. K. N. Panikkar and Sumit Sarkar.

Gupta reproduces whole texts of intelligence reports on the nexus between the RSS and the Mahasabha. The following three extracts are particularly revelatory:

> 1. A Note on the RSS in 1942 recorded: Dr B.S. Moonje, the acclaimed leader of the Hindu Mahasabha, frequently visited the Rashtriya Swayam Sewak Sangh volunteers and repeatedly told them that Hindustan belonged to the Hindus and that it should be retaken from the British.[41]

> 2. A Note on the RSS dated November 30, 1943 noted: Further evidence is available of the Hindu Mahasabha sympathy and support for the R.S.S.S. movement. Mention has already been made of the visit to the Poona Camp of V.D. Savarkar. He also inspected about 500 members of the Sangh and the Rashtriya Sewak Samiti at Amraoti on August 1st and urged them to strive for Hindu unity. It is significant that the Sangh's collections in Badaun for Bengal famine relief were said to be particularly interested in furthering the growth of the Sangh. (On the other hand, it was reported in August last that since the Delhi branch had for various reasons refused to identify itself with the Mahasabha, the latter had adopted a somewhat hostile attitude towards the Sangh and had refused permission to hold daily parades in the Mahasabha Bhawan.)[42]

Such isolated differences are now being cited to show that the two were at loggerheads. Ergo, Savarkar and the RSS differed and Godse did not belong to the RSS. Turf wars were inevitable, rather like lovers' quarrels.

> 3. The Intelligence Bureau's Note on the RSS dated, May 18, 1942 said: Its [RSS] real purpose is the attainment of 'Hindustan for the Hindus'; to this end it seeks to unify the

Hindus, imbue them with a martial spirit, impart military training, build up physique and character and establish a strong and disciplined Hindu militia. It aims at achieving ultimately an India free from both foreign and Muslim domination. Every candidate for admission to the Sangh is made to take the following secret oath standing under the flag of the organization:

'Before the All-Powerful God and my ancestors, I most solemnly take this oath, that I become a member of the Rashtriya Swayam Sewak Sangh in order to gain freedom for the Hindu nation by keeping intact my sacred Hindu religion, Hindu society and Hindu culture. I shall perform the work of the Sangh honestly, disinterestedly, with my heart and soul and I shall adhere to this oath all my life.

'Jai-Bajrang-Bali-Balbhim-ki-Jai'. . . .

A few days later, on November 13th, 1939 Dr N.D. Savarkar, brother of V.D. Savarkar, told 300 Rashtria Swayam Sewak Sangh volunteers at Nagpur that they were the allies of the Hindu Sabha and the Arya Samaj in the fight against the enemies of Hinduism *viz.*, the British Government, the Muslims and the Congress. During 1940, speakers continued to draw attention to the communal nature of the Sangh and emphasized its aims to protect Hinduism and prepare a useful potential force to deal with an expected Muslim invasion on the attainment of 'Swaraj'. Addressing meetings in the Bombay Province in November 1940 Professor M.S. Golwalkar, the present chief organizer of the Sangh, propounded the pan-Hindu theory of one undivided India under the Hindu rule of the Mahasabha. . . .

*Policy* – The policy of the Sangh is influenced to a considerable extent by its association with the Hindu Mahasabha. Exactly how closely the Sangh is connected with the Hindu Mahasabha is not known, as no public reference to its association is ever made by the leaders of either organization. That it is close, however, is clear from the respect with which Hindu Mahasabha leaders such as V.D.

Savarkar and Dr B.S. Moonje are treated by the Sangh and the authority with which they make public pronouncements regarding the Sangh. It is also significant that when Dr Hedgewar died, V.D. Savarkar, as president of the Hindu Mahasabha, instructed Hindu Sabhas throughout India to observe June 30th, 1942, as a day of mourning for him. It is, therefore necessary to bear in mind that any radical change in the declared policy of the Hindu Mahasabha will probably affect the policy of the Sangh.

In 1939 a reliable report stated that the leaders of the Sangh were not in favour of taking part in any political activities for some years to come as they were of opinion that to take part in any such activity prematurely would mean an end of the institution. Further, the policy of the Sangh was to prepare the Hindu youth for the future struggle for freedom of the country. They had no faith in democracy and believed that freedom could only be won by violence. . . .

If at any time in the future the Sangh or its political mentor, the Hindu Mahasabha, should decide to follow a policy which would bring them into conflict with Government the leaders of the Sangh would have at their disposal large numbers of well-disciplined and fairly well-trained officers and men capable, as recent years have shown, of rapidly increasing their numbers by training fresh recruits. Apart from repeated disregard of the ban on drill and uniform and occasional precipitation in communal trouble there has hitherto been nothing particularly objectionable about the Sangh's activities, but it is obvious that dangerous potentialities exist. It has been suggested in some quarters that the Sangh has pro-Japanese tendencies. Evidence of this is very scanty and by no means convincing. The most that can be said at present is that the Sangh might be drawn into pro-Japanese through its connection with the All-India Hindu Mahasabha, if the latter itself initiates or develops such activities.[43]

### Political irrelevance

Politically, by the mid-forties, Savarkar was a spent force. The Head of the Political Department in the India Office, John Percival Gibson minuted on August 1, 1944 that 'he did not consider it necessary to acknowledge' a cable Savarkar had sent to the Secretary of State for India, Leopold S. Amery, on July 26, 1944. It claimed that the Mahasabha was 'the only all-India representative body of Hindus'.[44] Savarkar sought frantically to keep himself in the limelight by the means commonly adopted by fading politicians – a steady stream of statements to the press. To catch public attention, one finds Savarkar making more and more rabid statements. One such statement of May 14, 1944 asked 'the Hindu Sanghathnists' not to contribute to the Kasturba Gandhi Memorial Fund. This was not because he belittled her sacrifice, but because he hated her husband:

> The proposal is definite in one point at any rate, that it is to be handed over to Gandhiji. Consequently, it amounts to nothing but a new Congressite fund to fill up the empty pockets which once overflowed when the Tilak Fund poured in. The Congressites are welcome to contribute to this fund or any fund which they like. But they should not dupe the people by putting on a false label and call it a national fund and spend it entirely in propagating the Congress work which especially the Hindu Sanghathnists feel highly detrimental to Hindu interests as well. . . . Under Gandhiji's leadership the ahimsa, charkha, Hindu-Moslem unity and vote for the Congress cannot but be the chief planks on which he wants women also to work organisedly. We can have positive proof of them in the Ashrams conducted up to this time on those lines. Just as half of the Tilak-Swaraj fund to which the label, contributed largely was spent in vilifying and exterminating the Tilakite principles and parties, and nearly half of the sum went to enrich the Moslem purse to drive the propaganda for 'Khilafat,' which as predicted by the Hindu Sanghathnists proved a veritable 'Afat' for the Hindus, even so this fund labeled by the

> innocuous name as the Kasturba National Fund will make the Tilakite and Hindu Sanghathnists millions all over India to curse the day they contributed to it.[45]

Expectedly, Savarkar lauded the establishment of Israel. This was not because he loved the Jews, nor even because he hated the Arabs as such, but because most Arabs were *Muslims.* It is another matter that some of the ablest exponents of the Arabs cause, and especially of Palestine, have been Christian Arabs – Charles H. Malik, Edward Said and Hasnan Ashrawi – but for Savarkar Arab meant simply Muslim. On December 19, 1947 he said,

> I am glad to note that the overwhelming majority of the leading nations in the world should have recognized the claim of the Jewish People, to establish an Independent Jewish state in Palestine and should have promised armed assistance to get it realized. After centuries of sufferings, sacrifices and struggle the Jews will soon recover their national Home in Palestine which has undoubtedly been their Fatherland and Holyland. Well may they compare this event to that glorious day in their history when Moses led them out of the Egyptian bondage and wilderness and the promised land flowing with milk and honey came well within sight. . . .
>
> In justice, therefore, *the whole of Palestine ought to have been restored to the Jews.* But taking into consideration the conflict of self-interests of the powerful nations in the UNO, their support to the resuscitation of the Jewish State in a part of Palestine at any rate wherein they still happen to be in majority and which includes some of their prominent Holy Places constitutes an event of historical justice and importance.
>
> It is consequently to be regretted that the delegation which represented our Hindusthani Government in the UNO should have voted against the creation of the Jewish State. The speeches of Shrimati Vijayalaxmi in particular were justly ridiculed when she declaimed

> melodramatically that the Indian Government refused to stab the unity and integrity of the Palestine State in the back by carving out a separate Jewish State.[46]

Increasingly politically marginalized and irrelevant, Savarkar's cup of bitterness was filled to the brink. He was evidently seething with vengeance, an emotion that came naturally to him. And Gandhi, as always, was the prime object of his hate. On June 6, 1944, shortly before the Partition of India, he levelled this brazenly false charge against Gandhi:

> Had not Gandhiji himself conspired with the Ali Brothers to invite an invasion by the Pathans and to enthrone the Amir of Afghanistan as the Emperor of India? Had he not declared again in the year 1940 in writing and repeated it now and then that if the Nizam subduing the Hindu Princes and with the support of Frontier tribes took Delhi and became the ruler of India that would be a perfect home rule, a cent per cent Swaraj? Thus a Pathani or a Nizami Moslem Raj is to Gandhiji a cent per cent Swaraj.[47]

After the Partition Savarkar took leave of his senses quite comprehensively.

# 5 GANDHI'S MURDER

IN THE CASE of *Rex vs. Nathuram V. Godse and Others*, including Vinayak D. Savarkar, the accused were charged with conspiracy to murder Mohandas Karamchand Gandhi. In pursuance of the conspiracy, at about 5 p.m. on January 30, 1948, Godse fired from a pistol three shots, at point-blank range in quick succession, at Gandhi at his prayer meeting in the grounds of Birla House in New Delhi. Gandhi fell down uttering the words 'Hei Ram'. None had predicted it, a good few feared that that might well be the lot of a man who had fought against hate. Gandhi succumbed to the injuries he had sustained soon after he was taken to his room in Birla House. Godse was caught and put under arrest.

The First Information Report was lodged at the Tughlak Road Police Station by Nand Lal Mehta who happened to be present at the time at the prayer-platform. It was recorded in Urdu. At the police station Godse gave his age as twenty-five. He was in fact thirty-seven.

Suspicion of complicity in the crime fell instantly on Savarkar because of Godse's 'close relationship with Savarkar' as his brother Gopal Godse told Walter Andersen in an interview on May 13, 1969.[1] Savarkar and Godse had known each other since 1929. Savarkar's house was searched the very next day. As his biographer wrote: 'Nathuram Godse's *lieutenantship* [sic] was bound to recoil upon Savarkar.'[2]

In the early hours of February 5, Savarkar was put in detention under the Bombay Public Safety Measures Act, 1947. On

February 22, he wrote to the Commissioner of Police offering to give an undertaking to the Government that 'I shall refrain from taking part in any communal or political activity *for any period the Government may require* in case I am released on that condition.'[3]

It did not save him from prosecution which, he obviously knew, was imminent. The government had only to accept this humiliating and explicitly open-ended offer if its aims were political. They were not. The Commissioner of Police, J.S. Bharucha himself met Savarkar soon after the murder. Savarkar flatly denied that he had anything to do with Gandhi's murder. The astute police officer, however, sensed something fishy. Twenty years later, sitting on a 'Commission of Inquiry into conspiracy to murder Mahatma Gandhi', Justice Jivan Lal Kapur, a former Judge of the Supreme Court, recorded,

> From that Mr Bharucha concluded that there was something wrong. He immediately went and saw Mr Morarji Desai [Home Minister of Bombay] and told him that *he suspected Savarkar* and also told him what Savarkar had said to him. Mr Morarji Desai said to Bharucha, 'Why do you not arrest him?' At that time Savarkar was really ill and Mr Bharucha told Mr Morarji Desai about it. Till then Mr Bharucha did not know that Savarkar's house was being watched. It may here be remarked that Mr Nagarwala has deposed that Savarkar was feigning illness.[4]

### Advance information

Only 32, Jamshed D. Nagarvala was Deputy Commissioner of Police, Bombay, incharge of the Bombay Crime Investigation Department Special Branch's Sections One and Two. He was responsible for collecting political intelligence and enjoyed Morarji Desai's confidence. The Minister had summoned him on January 21 to meet him at the Bombay Central railway station because he had a piece of important information to give him. Desai had, in turn, received it from Prof. Jagdish Chandra Jain, Professor of Adhamagadhi and

Hindi at the Ruia College in Bombay. He has told his story in full in his book *I Could Not Save Bapu.*[5] Briefly, that he had helped a young refugee from Punjab, Madanlal Pahwa, and earned his trust. He revealed to Jain a plot to kill Gandhi. His 'Seth' (boss) was Vishnu R. Karkare who, like him, lived in Ahmednagar. Savarkar knew of his exploits 'Savarkar patted me on the back and asked me to carry on'. Jain was greatly disturbed. 'This young boy, goaded by others, might commit some act of violence. Moreover he had seen Savarkar and had obtained his blessings.' (p. 15).

Sure enough, on January 20, Madanlal ignited a gun cotton slab at the back of Birla House damaging a wall. He was caught immediately and arrested. His minders Nathuram Godse, Narayan D. Apte, Godse's close friend, Vishnu Karkare, Digambar R. Badge and Badge's servant, Shankar Kistayya, fled from the scene.

Jain's worst fears were confirmed when he read the news of this attempt in the newspapers the next day. He promptly reported all he knew to Morarji Desai and Prime Minister B.G. Kher (p. 42).[6] Both Desai and Jain gave evidence at the murder trial. On January 21 the Minister instructed Nagarvala to keep a watch on Savarkar's house, arrest Karkare immediately and 'find out as to who else were involved in this plot' (p. 80). Nagarwala himself admitted to the Kapur commission that 'the watch was not efficient.'

Why Gandhi's life was not protected and saved despite the advance information which became more definite in the next few days – at least a week before the dastardly crime – is beyond the purview of this book. Suffice it to say here that the able trial Judge, Judge Atma Charan, ICS, censured the authorities, the three Judges of the East Punjab High Court who heard the appeals – Justices A.N. Bhandari, Achru Ram and G.D. Khosla – blithely and irresponsibly exonerated them. Justice Kapur found crass culpability.[7] The Delhi Police was none too co-operative with the Bombay Police. On January 31, Nagarvala was appointed Superintendent of Police, Delhi, in addition to his own duties. Investigations exposed the conspiracy in all its ramifications. The identity of the conspirators was no longer secret. On March 11, Savarkar was placed under arrest by the Delhi Police under a warrant from the Presidency Magistrate, Delhi, on a charge of being a participant in the conspiracy to murder Gandhi.

On May 4, a Special Court, headed by Atma Charan, ICS, District and Sessions Judge, Kanpur was constituted. On May 13, the case of *Rex vs. Nathuram Godse* and eight others was referred to him for trial. Savarkar was listed as the seventh accused. Another, Digambar Ramchandra Badge, turned approved and was given pardon by the Court on June 21. He had declined to retain a lawyer and volunteered to make a true statement of the facts. He was cross-examined closely for over a week and was found by the Court to be a truthful witness.

The chargesheet against the accused was submitted to the Court on May 27, the day the trial proceedings began in the Red Fort, Delhi.

### The chargesheet

In Court, C.K. Daphtary, Advocate-General for Bombay, led for the prosecution. The Chief Prosecutor, however, was none other than Vallabhbhai Patel, Deputy Prime Minster and Union Home Minister. As the investigations proceeded, both Morarji Desai and Vallabhbhai Patel became convinced of Savarkar's complicity in the crime. Desai bitterly said on the floor of Bombay's Legislative Council on April 3, 1948 that Savarkar's 'past services are more than offset by the present disservice'.[8]

The chargesheet against Savarkar could not have been filed unless Patel was convinced of his guilt. He was, in his time, an ace criminal lawyer admired for his skills in cross-examination. Patel wrote to Prime Minister Jawaharlal Nehru on February 27, 1948, 'I have kept myself *almost in daily touch with the progress of the investigation* regarding Bapu's assassination case. I devote a large part of my evening to discussing with Sanjevi the day's progress and giving instructions to him on any points that arise'. His conclusion was *characteristically clear*:

> It was a fanatical wing of the Hindu Mahasabha *directly under Savarkar* that [hatched] the conspiracy and saw it through.

> ... Of course, his assassination was welcomed by those of the RSS and the Mahasabha who were strongly opposed to his way of thinking and to his policy. But beyond this, I do not think it is possible, on the evidence which has come before us, to implicate any other members of the RSS or the Hindu Mahasabha.[9]

Despite the evidence that had come to light, not to forget Savarkar's abject offer of an undertaking to quit politics, Shyama Prasad Mookerjee tried to throw his weight around to get Savarkar off the hook. On May 4, the very day the Special Court was set up, he wrote to Patel:

> I understand Savarkar's name is being mentioned in this connection. I do not know what evidence has been found against him. I have not the least doubt that you will satisfy yourself that nothing is done which may give rise to the suggestion later on that he was being prosecuted on account of his political convictions. I hope the records will be placed before you before any decision is taken. His sacrifices and suffering in the past have been considerable and unless there is some positive proof against him, he should not, at this age, be subjected to a charge of conspiracy to commit murder. I leave the matter to your decision.[10]

Patel promptly replied on May 6, 1948:

> As regards Savarkar, the Advocate-General of Bombay, who is in charge of the case, and other legal advisers and investigating officers met me at a conference in Delhi before I came here. I told them, quite clearly, that the question of inclusion of Savarkar must be approached purely from a legal and judicial standpoint and political considerations should not be imported into the matter. My instructions were quite definite and beyond doubt and I am sure they will be acted upon. I have also told them that, if they come to the view that Savarkar should be included, *the papers should*

> *be placed before me before action is taken.* This is, of course, in so far as the question of guilt is concerned from the point of view of law and justice. *Morally, it is possible that one's conviction may be the other way about.*[11]

Patel, as we noted above, was an extremely capable criminal lawyer. He knew his law and had perused the papers carefully. He knew that *the case against Savarkar hinged on the testimony of the approver, Digambar Badge,* an admitted accomplice. He had told the police and repeated to the court on oath that he had twice accompanied Godse and Apte to Savarkar Sadan in Bombay on January 14 and 17, that is shortly before Pahwa ignited the gun slab on January 20 and Godse committed the murder on January 30. On the second occasion, January 17, he heard Savarkar declaring while bidding them farewell, '*Yashasvi houn ya*' ('Be successful and return'). On the way back Apte told Badge that Savarkar had predicted that 'Gandhiji's 100 years were over. There was no doubt that the work would be successfully finished'.

Patel knew, of course, that this by itself did not suffice to warrant a conviction. Corroboration was necessary. There was corroborative material before him, of course. But it all depended on what the Court thought of it – in the light of the law. *Morally* he had no doubt as to Savarkar's guilt as his letter to Nehru reveals. Even the Judge certified that Badge was a truthful witness, unshaken by the cross-examination.

### Rule of law, rule of prudence

That the evidence of an accomplice who turns approver requires corroboration is not strictly a rule of law. It is, rather, a rule of prudence. It has ripened into a rule of law over the years. It is based on the rule that while judgment in a civil case must rest on a balance of probabilities, guilt in a criminal case must be proved beyond reasonable doubt. It used to be said then that it is better to let ten guilty persons escape rather than allow one innocent person to be convicted.

That masterpiece of simple, elegant legislation drafted by Sir James Fitzames Stephen, the Indian Evidence Act, 1872, says, in Section 114:

> The Court may presume the existence of any fact which it thinks likely to have happened, regard being had to the common course of natural events, human conduct and public and private business, in their relation to the facts of the particular case.

Rather unusually in a statute, the Section proceeds to provide nine explanatory 'illustrations':

> The Court may presume . . . (b) that an accomplice is unworthy of credit, unless he is corroborated in material particulars. . . . But the Court shall also have regard to such facts as the following, in considering whether such maxims do or do not apply to the particular case before it. . . . As to illustration (b) – A, a person of the highest character, is tried for causing a man's death by an act of negligence in arranging certain machinery. B, a person of equally good character, who also took part in the arrangement, describes precisely what was done, and admits and explains the common carelessness of A and himself. This is not all. It goes on to add, 'as to illustration (b) – a crime is committed by several persons. A, B and C, three of the criminals, are captured on the spot and kept apart from each other. Each gives an account of the crime implicating D, and the accounts corroborate each other in such a manner as to render previous concert highly improbably.

Thus the caution in illustration (b) is qualified by these two cases. For good measure, Section 133 lays down that 'an accomplice shall be a competent witness against an accused person, and a conviction is not illegal merely because it proceeds upon thc uncorroborated testimony of an accomplice'.

Such is the letter of the law. The rulings of the Privy Council and of the Supreme Court built up a body of case law which established that independent corroboration in respect of material particulars is necessary, albeit not every material particular. Were it not for the tapes, Richard Nixon would have gone scot free. King Henry II of England could not have been charged with instigating the murder of Becket even though the instigation was clear: 'Who will free me from this turbulent priest?' and, more provocatively, 'What a parcel of fools and dastards have I nourished in my house, that not one of them will avenge me of this one upstart clerk?'

In his judgment dated February 10, 1949, Judge Atma Charan acquitted Savarkar. He found Badge to be a truthful witness but held the corroborative evidence was vague and inadequate. A conviction, in the circumstance, would be 'unsafe' he ruled. Twenty years later, on September 30, 1969, Justice Jivan Lal Kapur, as Commission of Inquiry, concluded emphatically in his Report after a rigorous analysis of evidence that 'all these facts taken together were destructive of any theory other than the conspiracy to murder by Savarkar and his group.'[12] Patel was vindicated. The matter does not rest there. The Commission had before it evidence which was not tendered before the Court, perhaps because it could not be. *It included the testimony of Savarkar's aides given after his death.* They deposed to the visits of Godse and Apte on which the Court found the evidence in corroboration to be weak and vague. *If these aides had deposed in court, Savarkar could not have escaped conviction for the crime.* More on that, presently.

### Protecting the mentor

Even in 1948, two incontrovertible facts sufficed to damn Savarkar in the eyes of all right thinking persons. In any case of conspiracy, the relationship between the accused is a fact of crucial importance. So is the conduct of the accused.

Every single accused was out to protect Savarkar. Godse lied as freely in court as he did at the police station about his age. He denied that any conspiracy existed and said that 'the events upto 20$^{th}$ January 1948 are quite independent and they have no connection whatsoever with what happened thereafter and on 30th January, 1948'.[13] Godse said:

> I have worked for several years in RSS and subsequently joined the Hindu Mahasabha and volunteered myself to fight as a soldier under its pan-Hindu flag. About this time Veer Savarkar was elected to the Presidentship of the Hindu Mahasabha. The Hindu Sanghatan Movement got verily electrified and vivified as never before, under his magnetic lead and whirl-wind propaganda. Millions of Hindu Sanghatanists looked up to him as the chosen hero, as the ablest and most faithful advocate of Hindu cause. I too was one of them. I worked devotedly to carry on the Mahasabha activities and hence came to be personally acquainted with Savarkarji. . . . But it must be specially noted that these, *our casual visits to Savarkar Sadan* were *restricted generally* to this Hindu Sanghatan office, situated on the ground floor, for the above mentioned reasons. Veer Savarkar was residing on the first floor of the house. It was only very rarely that we could interview Veer Savarkar personally and that too by special appointment.

This was false. Mass of evidence surfaced to show that Godse and Apte had *unrestricted* access to Savarkar. Godse added that in 1947 'we felt in our heart of hearts that time had come when we should bid goodbye to Veer Savarkar's lead and cease to consult him in our *future policy and programme.* Nor should we *confide in him our future plans*' (pp. 20–21). This protective lie was repeated for emphasis: 'We resolved not to confide any of our new plans to any of them including Veer Savarkar. . . . I re-assert that it is not true that Veer Savarkar had any knowledge of my activities which ultimately led me to fire shots at Gandhiji' (p. 24).

We noted in chapter 1 above M.R. Jayakar's disgust at the undignified conduct of G.D. Savarkar at his trial, in contrast to the heroic stand by freedom-fighters. Let alone heroism, even a modicum of truth was untraceable in Savarkar's written statement in Court. Robert Payne is right in observing that Savarkar

> went to extraordinary lengths to deny that he had anything to do with the conspiracy. He had never met the conspirators; if he did, then the meeting had nothing to do with the conspiracy; he never came down the stairs; if he did, and if he spoke the parting words, 'Be successful and come back,' then it must be understood that he was talking about something entirely remote from the conspiracy such as the sale of shares of Hindu Rashtra or civil resistance to the government of the Nizam of Hyderabad or any one of a hundred legitimate undertakings. So he went on, examining each word he was supposed to have said in purely legalistic terms as though he were remote from the conflict. The circumstantial evidence was impressive, the story told by Badge was a convincing one. Savarkar took each sentence out of its context and showed that it was devoid of any precise meaning.[14]

The nadir was reached in the brazen falsehood to which he stooped in describing his relationship with Godse and Apte. Savarkar's statement on this aspect *is quoted in extenso*:

> Through my organizational correspondence, tours, writings and speeches I came into personal contact with thousands of leaders, workers and members of Mahasabha all over India.
>
> It was as one of these numerous Hindu Mahasabha workers and volunteers that Pandit Nathuram Godse *got himself specially introduced* to me. Mr Apte also *got introduced to me by a letter* stating that he was a Hindu Sabha worker at Nagar and meant to start a Rifle Club, which the Collector had given him permission to start. Dr Parchure also *got himself introduced* to me as the leader of the Gwalior Hindu Sabha. I heard of Mr Badge when he wrote to me that he was a Hindu Sanghatanist worker and sold arms which according to law could be sold without licence. The other accused Shankar, Gopal Godse and Madanlal were never known to me, nor had I ever heard of them. . . . Mr Apte

> and Pandit Godse got themselves introduced to me as Hindu Sabha workers at Nagar and Poona and later on came to be personally acquainted with me.[15]

### The acolyte

After Savarkar's death, Godse's brother, Gopal, revealed the closeness of the relationship in his Marathi book *Gandhi Hatya, Ani Mee* ('Gandhi's Murder and I') published in 1967. An English translation was published later.[16] Gopal Godse's revelations about their revelation totally belie Savarkar's version. It was much more than an 'acquaintance'. It was a close relationship between mentor and disciple. They met first *in 1929* when Godse's father was transferred to Ratnagiri where Savarkar resided. 'Just three days after we reached Ratnagiri Nathuram had gone to pay a visit to Veer Savarkar, for the first time. Thereafter he went to him often' (p. 109). Godse undertook to copy Savarkar's writings for him.

> Nathuram agreed with the stand of the RSS. The Patit Pawan Mandir of Ratnagiri was a structure of brick and stone and its influence was confined to its environments and to its limited surrounding area. The RSS however, was a temple without a structure, yet it could accommodate all the Hindus, to whatever place they might belong. Entire India was its proposed field of work, and as it had vowed to make the nation strong the attainment of independence formed a part of that vow. He could also see the branches of the RSS slowly growing in number.
>
> A branch of the RSS was opened at Sangli headed by Shree Kashinathpant Limaye. Nathuram began to take part in the Sangh activities most assiduously. Very soon he came to head its academic department (as 'Baudhik Karyawaha').
>
> At this time Veer Savarkar was writing articles, in the 'Kirloskar' Magazine, criticizing the inconsistent, narrow-minded and harmful traditions in the Hindu society. With *his daily personal contact* with Veer Savarkar, Nathuram

> had become quite familiar with his strictly logical approach to any problem and so these articles influenced him all the more. (p. 114)

So much for the casual 'got introduced' pretext.

Once Savarkar was set free in 1937, 'Nathuram started going about with Veer Savarkar everywhere' (p. 16). He launched a journal *Agrani* which was renamed *Hindu Rashtra.* Keer records:

> In his early youth Godse was a worker of the RSS and later, he was a prominent member of the All-India Committee of the Hindu Mahasabha. He was a well-known journalist in Maharashtra and the editor of a Marathi Daily, the Agrani, – the Leader – changed to a new name, the Hindu Rashtra at a later stage. Better known as Pandit Nathuram Godse, this editor was a staunch Savarkarite, and *was fairly known as the vanguard and lieutenant of Savarkar.*[17]

He however qualified this by retailing Godse's false tale of revolt.[18]

Collins and Lapierre, who had access to police records, wrote, 'No leader ever had a more devoted acolyte. Godse followed Savarkar across India'.[19] They added: 'Very few people had the right to move immediately past that room [the guards] up a flight of stairs to the personal quarters of the dictator of the Hindu Rashtra Dal. Nathuram Godse and Narayan Apte were among them. Digambar Badge was not and so . . . they went upstairs without him.'[20]

### 'Veer' Savarkar?

The adjective 'brave', 'veer', is commonly prefaced to Savarkar's name. Yet, how brave really was the man? It is revealing to contrast Savarkar's conduct in this case with that of any of the heroes in the freedom movement whether in India or elsewhere – an abject undertaking to abjure politics for as long as the State wishes; if need be, for the rest of his life; the lie, brazen and demeaning; and, a written statement with alternative defences in the manner of common accused in the dock. Where was the bravery in the face of adversity? It was never evident – whether in 1911, 1917, 1925, 1948 or in 1950. We shall return to this presently.

Revelations by another admirer confirm the impressions one gets from the trial proceedings. P.L. Inamdar was an able lawyer who defended Dattatraya Sadashiv Parchure and Gopal Godse in the trial Court and on appeal. He won an acquittal for Parachure in the High Court. His memoirs reflect modesty, a trait rare in such writings. Inamdar was an ardent admirer of Savarkar. The chapter on Savarkar in his memoirs is all the more damning for that and for the author's careful statement of the facts. Consider these excerpts, which reveal nothing but a callous and self-centred personality.

> During the whole of the trial, I never saw Savarkar turning his head towards even Nathuram, who used to sit by him, in fact next to him, much less speak with him. While the other accused freely talked to each other exchanging notes or banter, Savarkar sat there sphinx-like in silence, completely ignoring his co-accused in the dock, in an unerringly disciplined manner. He did not talk to me in Court during the whole of the trial, except once. He had, I thought, perhaps resolved to act in court, his defence against the charge of conspiracy with Nathuram or with any one of the accused and, in fact, to perform his role demonstratively, even with respect to the counsels of the other accused.
>
> During the various talks I had with Nathuram, he told me that he was deeply hurt by this – Tatyarao's [Savarkar's] calculated, demonstrative non-association with him either in court or in the Red Fort Jail during all the days of the Red Fort Trial. How Nathuram yearned for a touch of Tatyarao's hand, a word of sympathy, or at least a look of compassion in the secluded confines of the cells. Nathuram referred to his hurt feelings in this regard even during my last meeting with him at the Simla High Court.[21]

Robert Payne was not the only one to write contemptuously

of Savarkar's written statement in court in his defence. So did Inamdar whose words carry greater weight. He was an eye witness to the act which Savarkar put on.

> Savarkar had prepared a written statement in defence of his case replete with appendices of newspaper cuttings and he read out the statement in the Court with all the gimmicks of an orator bemoaning his fate of being charged with the murder of Mahatmaji by the independent Indian Government, when he had admired and eulogized the personality of the Mahatmaji so sincerely and so often. Savarkar actually wiped his cheeks in court while reading this part of his oration. . . .
>
> Savarkar claimed that he was wholly innocent of the crime! I am alive to the stage of his career at which Savarkar then was. But believe me, Savarkar was very nervous and was getting more and more agitated as the trial progressed.[22]

It may be noted that *the exclamation mark is in the original.*

Savarkar went so far once, in September 1948, as to solicit Inamdar's professional help, to his great embarrassment. The Court accorded its permission for the visit. Savarkar's lawyer, L.B. Bhopatkar, himself conveyed Savarkar's request to the impeccably proper Inamdar,

> He repeatedly asked me if he would be acquitted and wanted me to assure him sincerely. What I noted was that he did not ask me a single question about the case against my clients Dr Parchure and Gopal Godse or about any of the other accused including Nathuram, nor any question about me personally. I spent nearly three hours with him.[23]

On the last day of the trial Savarkar refused to sign his autograph on a new autograph book which Inamdar had bought and asked him to buy for himself, instead, any of his books which bore his signature. When he went to see Savarkar after the High

Court's judgment, he declined to meet Inamdar. The astute Inamdar does not conceal a shrewd assessment of the man beneath the mask – the nervousness born out of deep consciousness of guilt and, with it, a dread of imprisonment he had sought unsuccessfully to ward off by offering to quit politics altogether leaving the cause of Hindutva for braver men to espouse. The annals of great trials provide hardly a parallel in cowardice and deceit.

### The murder

Savarkar's conduct, thought very relevant, does not dispense with the need to analyse the record of the trial so far as it concerns him in the context of the prosecution case on the conspiracy. Godse owned up responsibility for the murder, denied any conspiracy. The sole issue, therefore, was the existence of the conspiracy and the identity of the conspirators.

Accused in the case were Nathuram Godse (aged 37), Narayan Apte (34), editor and printer respectively of *Hindu Rashtra* at Poona, Vishnu Karkare (38), who ran a hotel in Ahmednagar, Madanlal Pahwa (20), Shankar Kistayya (20), Gopal Godse (27), V.D. Savarkar (65), and Dattatraya Parchure (47), a medical practitioner in Gwalior. Shankar Kistayya was a servant of the approver Digambar Badge (39) who had received pardon. Barring Kistayya, all were committed Mahasabhaites blindly loyal to Savarkar.

The prosecution case was well summed up in the Kapur Report from which this resume is drawn.[24] A conspiracy to murder Mahatma Gandhi was entered into sometime in December 1947. Parchure, it was alleged, joined the conspiracy on January 27, 1948. In furtherance of the object of the conspiracy, Badge and Shankar brought two gun cotton slabs and five hand-grenades with primers and detonators to Bombay on the evening of January 14, 1948 which were kept at the residence of Dikshitji Maharaj with a servant of his. Apte and Nathuram Godse arrived at Bombay the same evening, and went to the house of Dikhshitji Maharaj with Badge to procure a revolver from him but could not get one. Karkare and Madanlal had arrived in Bombay sometime earlier and were staying in Hindu Mahasabha Bhawan where Badge and Shankar also stayed. On the

15$^{th}$ the explosives kept at the house of Dixitji Maharaj were taken over by Karkare and Madanlal and were brought to Delhi the same evening tied up in a bedding. Badge and Nathuram Godse returned to Poona – Badge in order to make arrangement about his bhandar and Nathuram to fetch his brother Gopal Godse who had promised to provide him with a revolver. Badge and Shankar returned to Bombay reaching there early on the morning of the 17$^{th}$. Evidently, Apte and Nathuram Godse were also in Bombay and they collected some money for expenses required to carry out their plot. Nathuram Godse and Apte left by plane *on the afternoon of the 17$^{th}$* arriving at Delhi in the evening and stayed at the Marina Hotel, then a fairly posh European style hotel in Connaught Circus. They had met Savarkar that day. Madanlal and Karkare had arrived the same day at about 12.30 p.m. and not being able to get accommodation at the Hindu Mahasabha Bhawan stayed at the Shariff Hotel.

Badge and Shankar arrived at Delhi on the evening of the 19$^{th}$ and stayed at the Hindu Mahasabha Bhawan. Gopal Godse arrived at Delhi sometime after 17$^{th}$ January. One account was that he arrived on the evening of 18$^{th}$ January and met the others on 19$^{th}$ January. He also stayed at Hindu Mahasabha Bhawan. Thus, Badge, Shankar, Gopal Godse and Madanlal stayed at the Hindu Mahasabha Bhawan for the night. Apte and Badge and Shankar went to the Birla House on the morning of the 20$^{th}$ and made a survey of the prayer ground and the back of the servants quarters and then returned to the Hindu Mahasabha Bhawan. In the jungle behind the Bhawan they tried out the two revolvers that they had brought but they were found to be unserviceable.

Thereafter they all met at the Marina Hotel in Nathuram's room and the plan for the evening was finalized which was that Madanlal should explode the gun-cotton slab at the back of the Birla House in order to create a commotion and taking advantage of the panic thus caused, Badge and Shankar would fire at Mahatma Gandhi with the two revolvers and would also throw at him a hand-grenade each. Badge was to fire the revolver and throw a hand-grenade from the trellis work of the window of the room in the servants quarter immediately behind where Mahatmaji used to sit at the time of the prayers. He was to enter the room posing as a photographer with the object of taking a photograph of the prayer meeting. Gopal Godse, Madanlal and Karkare were to throw the remaining hand-grenades at the same time. Apte and Nathuram were to give signals for the various participants to carry out their respective and assigned parts. In pursuance of this plan, the gun cotton slab and a hand-grenade were given to Madanlal, one hand-grenade and revolver to Badge, one hand-grenade each to Gopal Godse and Karkare. The conspirators then left the Marina Hotel for Birla House, Madanlal and Karkare first, all the others excepting Nathuram Godse a little later in a taxi. Nathuram was to follow them. Madanlal ignited the gun-cotton slab on the wall near the back gate of Birla House but the others did not carry out their respective assigned parts. Nathuram Godse, Apte and Gopal Godse left immediately in the taxi by which they had come. Madanlal was arrested on the spot. Karkare, Badge and Shankar managed to escape.

While Nathuram Godse and Apte were in Bombay they had unsuccessfully tried to get a pistol from Dadaji Maharaj and Dixitji Maharaj. From Delhi they went to Gwalior arriving at 10.30 p.m. on 27th January and stayed the night and the day following with Dr Parchure to whom they disclosed their plan and with his help and with that of Dandwate (the absconding accused) they were able to get a pistol from one Goel. Leaving Gwalior the same night they arrived at Delhi the next morning where they were joined by Karkare and three of them spent the night in the retiring room at the Delhi Main Railway Station. The next evening, on January 30, Nathuram Godse shot Mahatma Gandhi dead and was arrested at the spot.

The Special Judge found seven of the accused guilty and sentenced two, Nathuram Godse and Apte, to be hanged, and the rest to transportation for life. Savarkar was acquitted. On appeal to the High Court, two more were acquitted, i.e. Parchure and Shankar Kishtayya. Appeal of the rest of the accused persons were dismissed, the sentences of death on Nathuram Godse and Apte were confirmed. Sentences passed on the other three were upheld.

Nathuram Godse and Apte were hanged in Ambala Jail on November 15, 1949. Ultimately, on October 12, 1964, Gopal Godse, Karkare and Madanlal were released from jail by the Government of India although the Government of Maharashtra was not in favour of the release and had so advised the Government of India. Gulzari Lal Nanda was then Union Home Minister.

Along with the rest, Savarkar was charged with conspiracy to murder Gandhi under Section 120B (conspiracy) of the Indian Penal Code read with Section 302 (murder) of the Code. Other accused faced charges under the Code, the Indian Arms Act and the Explosive Substances Act.

### The approver

As in many cases of conspiracy, an accomplice spilled the beans and received pardon on the assurance that he would testify truthfully in court. Digambar Badge was praised by Judge Atma Charan. He figured as Prosecution Witness 57 and his evidence comes on pages 80 to 118 of the Printed Record, from July 20 to July 30, 1948. He lived in Pune and was a dealer in arms and ammunition. 'From the middle of 1947, I was dealing in cartridges, bombs, rifles, sten guns, etc. . . . I used to sell daggers, knives, tiger-claws, knuckle-dusters, pen-knives, axes etc. I used to sell books. I know the institution known as Hindu Mahasabha' since 1940. He attended its annual session every year. 'Whenever I attended any such session I used to sell weapons and books there'. He ran the Shastra Bhandar. By all tests, he was a most useful member of the conspiracy. He knew Appa Kasar, Savarkar's body guard, since 1944. 'I had dealings with him in daggers'. Savarkar's secretary, Gajanadrao Damle, was another acquaintance. Badge was introduced to Savarkar in 1944–45. Godse he knew since 1940–41. The first arms deal with Apte and Karkare was in July–August 1947. In November came a pressing demand for arms. Eventually it was arranged that delivery would be made at the Mahasabha office in Bombay.

Badge arrived there with all the 'stuff' on January 14, 1948. Moments after they met that day in Bombay, Apte, Godse and Badge went to Savarkar Sadan with a khaki cloth bag containing 2 gun-cotton slabs, 5 hand-grenades, fuse wire, detonators, etc. 'On reaching Savarkar Sadan, Apte asked me to wait outside it. Apte took the bag from my hand, and then Apte and Godse went inside

Savarkar Sadan. They came back 5–10 minutes later. Apte had the bag with him when he came out.' They returned to the Mahasabha office. Obviously, Badge had no interest in embroidering his account.

Apte asked Karkare and Madanlal to proceed to Delhi with the bag.

> Apte asked me if I was prepared to go with them to Delhi. I asked him as to what was the work at Delhi. Apte told me that Tatyarao [Savarkar] had decided that Gandhiji, Jawahar Lal Nehru and Suhrawardy should be 'finished' and had entrusted that work to them. He further told me that for that purpose I should accompany them to Delhi and that they would meet funds towards my travelling expenses. I say that I was willing to proceed to Delhi but could not proceed immediately as I would have to go back to Poona to make arrangements regarding my house-hold affairs. Nathuram Godse thereon said that he also wanted to go to Poona to meet his brother Gopal Godse, who had undertaken to make arrangements for procuring a revolver, and to bring him down to Bombay for accompanying them to Delhi.

Badge traced their movements in detail and his meetings with other conspirators like Madanlal. Money was never a problem for Savarkar. He was funded by noted industrialists like Gulabchand Hirachand[25] and lived in comfort – unlike the freedom fighters. The other conspirators also found it easy to raise funds.

Badge returned to Bombay on January 17 and met Godse and Apte at the Victoria Terminus Railway Station.

> When we had gone a few paces Apte suggested that before proceeding to Delhi we should collect some funds. Apte brought a taxi and we sat down in it. We then proceeded to Bombay Dyeing House which is on the Government Gate Road at Lal Bagh. We then met Seth Charandas Meghji Mathuradas. He is the Proprietor of the Bombay Dyeing works. I knew him from before. I then introduced Apte and Godse to him. There was then a conversation among those

> three persons. We three then proceeded to the Hindu Mahasabha Office at Dadar. We had proceeded there with a view to picking up Shankar. When Shankar sat down in the car, Godse suggested that we should go to take the last 'Darshan' of Tatyarao. We then proceeded to Savarkar Sadan at Shivaji Park. The taxi halted at the crossing of the main road with the lane that leads to the house of Savarkar. His house would be at a distance of 30–40 paces from the crossing. We got down from the taxi, and walked down to the house of Savarkar. Shankar was asked to wait outside the compound of Savarkar Sadan.
>
> Apte, Godse and I entered the compound of that house. Apte asked me to wait in the room on the ground floor. Nathuram Godse and Apte then went up. They came down after 5–10 minutes. Godse and Apte as they came down the stairs were followed immediately by Tatyarao. Tatyarao said 'be successful and come'. Note – the exact words used are '*Yashasvi houn ya*'. Tatyarao had addressed these words to Apte and Godse. We four then got into the taxi and proceeded towards the Ruia College. Apte said in the taxi that Tatyarao had predicted that Gandhiji's hundred years were over. Apte further said that there was no doubt that our work would be successfully finished. Note - the exact words used are '*Tatyaravani ase bhavishya kale ahe ki Gandhijichi sambhar varshe bharali – ata apale kam nishchita honar yat kahi sanshya nahi*'. We then proceeded to the house of Shrimant Afzulpurkar.

Badge narrated the trip to Delhi on January 19, the familiarizing visit to Birla House the next morning, with Apte, the explosion that evening, their flight from Delhi and arrival in Poona on January 22. He was arrested at dawn on January 31. 'I was given to understand by Apte that Tatyarao (Savarkar) had given orders to carry out the mission. I took it to be a command from Tatyarao and thus bound to carry it out. Ever since I got acquainted with Nathuram Godse and Apte I did whatever they asked me to do.'

Savarkar was accused No. 7 but his lawyer was the first to

cross-examine Badge. It drew from him fulsome praise for Savarkar and his writings.

> I did not sell any books issued by the Congress. . . . I have been to Savarkar Sadan several times but I met him [Savarkar] only once.
>
> The entrance door to the house of Savarkar is visible from outside the boundary wall as the door is at a higher level. The gate leading to the compound is at one side of the boundary wall. If one stands at the gate one would not be able to see the entrance-door leading to the house of Savarkar. The house is double-storeyed. I cannot say if some tenants reside in the house. Some persons other than the members of the family of Savarkar do reside in the house. I had met Tatyarao Savarkar on the ground floor of his house. It is true that as one enters the house A.S. Bhide resides towards the left of the house. I cannot say in what portion of the house Damle lives. He is always to be found in that house. There is a room facing the entrance-door. A table with newspapers is kept there. There are also two chairs kept there. There is a piece of wooden plank fixed to the wall. A telephone is kept over the plank. It is true that Tatyarao lives on the first-floor. The reading-room is not open to members of the public.

He added:

> I remember 15th August 1947 when the independence of India was celebrated. Savarkar had hoisted the Hindu Mahasabha and the National flags that day at his house. I had hoisted the Hindu Mahasabha flag only that day at my house. I had not seen any Hindu Mahasabhaite except Tatyarao Savarkar flying the National flag at his house that day. The Hindu Mahasabhaites whom I had seen had just flown the Hindu Mahasabha flag at their houses that day. It is true that it had been decided by the Bombay Provincial Hindu Sabha that only 'Bhagwa' was to be flown that day. It

> is a fact that the Hindu Mahasabhaites had resented the flying of the National flag at his house by Tatyarao Savarkar against the resolution passed by the working committee. I had also resented to his flying the National flag at his house. Nathuram Godse, Apte and Karkare had also resented to his flying the National flag at his house.

> The evidence showed that the relations remained as close.

> I came to know Dixit Maharaj in 1940–41. He is a religious head, and is a Sanatanist. I cannot say whether he is a Congressite. I used to go to the house of Dixit Maharaj as he used to purchase weapons from me. I never put any question to him as to why he wanted weapons from me. He used to purchase weapons from me only during the Hindu-Muslim riots. I only sell weapons to Hindus. Dixit Maharaj used to purchase daggers, knuckle dusters, and tiger claws.

Savarkar's was the longest cross-examination. Lawyers for the rest were brief. The prosecution produced two witnesses to corroborate Badge's evidence on the visits to Savarkar's house. One was an actress Modak (PW. 60) whose film name was Bimba. She met Apte and Godse on the Poona Express bound for Bombay on January 14. As they alighted at the Dadar Railway Station she was received by her brother there and they offered Godse and Apte a lift to the Shivaji Park.

> My brother's house and the Savarkar-Sadan are situated on the same road and on the same side of the road. There is an open space between the two houses. If one comes from towards the Dadar Railway station and turns into the road the house in which my brother lives comes first and the Savarkar-Sadan, thereafter. The two houses would be on the right-hand side of the road. We passed and house in which my brother lives, and stopped the car opposite the Savarkar-Sadan. The two gentlemen got down. We then went ahead to turn the car and bring it back to my brother's house. I

> saw the two gentlemen heading towards the Savarkar-Sadan. I identified both these gentlemen in an identification-parade held before a Magistrate at Bombay. I first saw them on 14th January, 1948, then in the identification parade and now in Court. I had not seen them otherwise on any other occasion.

The other witness was Aitappa Kotian, the taxi driver, who drove Godse, Apte and Badge to Savarkar Sadan on January 17. He identified them in the identification parade and in court as well. So also, Badge's servant Kistayya.

> I was then asked to take the taxi to the Shivaji Park. I started the taxi and took it along the Ranade Road. I took the taxi that way to the Shivaji Park – southside. I then stopped the taxi at the intersection of the second road on the south side of the Shivaji Park. The four passengers got down from the taxi there. So far as I could see they went up to the second house from the corner of the road on my right. They came back to the taxi in about five minutes time. I was then asked to take them to the Hindu Colony at Dadar. When I reached the Ruia College they asked a man there for Dr Maheshaiskar's Wadi. He asked them to go ahead so far as the Irani shop and said that the 'Wadi' was situated behind it. I took the taxi there and they all got down. They then entered a building and came back after about 15 minutes' time. I was then asked take them to Kurla.

He narrated in detail how he earned good money by the many excursions on which he drove these passengers.

### Savarkar's version

Savarkar's version on the two visits merits quotation *in extensor* in fairness. On Godse, Apte and Badge's visit at 9 p.m. on January 14, he said:

> Firstly herein Badge makes no mention anywhere of my name, so it only comes to this that Apte and Godse visited Savarkar Sadan for 5 or 10 minutes. But visiting Savarkar Sadan does not necessarily mean visiting Savarkar. Apte and Godse were well acquainted with Damle, Bhide and Kasar who were always found there on the ground floor and Bhide and Damle resided there. These facts Badge himself has told in his evidence. So Apte and Godse might have gone to see their friends and co-workers in Hindu Mahasabha . . . or to the phone or to see those other workers of the Hindu Mahasabha who sat reading in the Reading Room, and both of them went out within 5 or 10 minutes.
>
> Badge clearly says that Apte had the bag with him when he came out. There is not a word said by Badge which can show that Apte went inside the house to keep the bag. Further on Badge clearly admits that the bag was kept by them in Dixit Maharaj's house that very night.
>
> Secondly, it should be noted moreover that both Apte and Godse deny it and state they never went with Badge and the bag to Savarkar Sadan as alleged. Thirdly, there is no independent evidence produced by the Prosecution to corroborate this incident. Consequently, this whole story of 'Badge and the bag' cannot have an evidentiary value at all.

Apte's conversation with Badge on January 15 was hearsay. Badge had not heard Savarkar himself on the plot to kill Gandhi.

> Secondly taking it for granted that Badge himself is telling the truth when he says Apte told him this sentence, the question still remains whether what Apte told Badge is true or false. There is no evidence to show that I had ever told Apte to finish Gandhi, Nehru and Suhrawardy. *Apte might have invented this wicked lie to exploit Savarkar's moral influence on Hindu Sanghatanists for his own purposes. It is the case of the prosecution itself that Apte was used to resort* [sic] *to such unscrupulous tricks.* For example, Apte is alleged to have given

false names and false addresses to hotel keepers and others and collected arms and ammunition secretly which were not allowed by the law to be sold or possessed without licenses.

Thirdly, both Apte and Godse deny emphatically the allegations that they had ever told Badge any such lies regarding me and that in order to save his skin and secure pardon as an approver Badge had told these lies to incriminate me under police pressure or to solicit their pleasure as he knew that the police were extremely anxious and desperately trying to get some evidence true or false to implicate me in this case.

Fourthly, from the Prosecution point of view this part of Badge's evidence is the only material part so far as I am concerned. But an approver's statements are not to be taken as reliable unless and until they are corroborated in material particulars by independent and good evidence. But this very part of Badge's evidence against me is not at all corroborated by any other independent and reliable evidence which the Prosecution could produce.

(F) The sixth incident as alleged by Badge took place on the 17th January, 1948. He says in his deposition on page 207 thus, 'Godse, Apte and myself (Badge) and Shankar took a taxi and drove. Godse said, let us have the last 'Darshan' of Tatyarao. We drove to Savarkar Sadan. Shankar was asked to wait outside the compound. We three entered Savarkar's house, Apte asked me (Badge) to wait in the room on the ground floor. Godse and Apte then went upstairs. They came down after 5 or 10 minutes. Godse and Apte, as they came upstairs were followed by Tatyarao immediately. Tatyarao said, 'Be successful and come back' (yashasvi houn ya). Tatyarao said these words to Apte and Godse. We four then got into the taxi leaving Savarkar's house and proceeded towards Ruia College. Apte told me in the taxi that Tatyarao had said that Gandhiji's hundred years were over. Apte further said that there was no doubt that our work would be successfully finished'. They then proceeded to the house of Afzulpurkar etc. etc.

Firstly, I submit in this respect that *Apte and Godse did not see me on 17th January, 1948 or on any other day near about* and I did not say to them. 'Be successful and come back' and I had never predicted that Gandhiji's hundred years were over, to Apte or to any one else.

Secondly, assuming that what Badge says about the visit is true, still as he clearly admits that he sat in the room on the ground floor of my house and Apte and Godse alone went upstairs, he could not have known for certain whether they could or did see me at all or returned after meeting someone of the family of the tenant who also resided on the first floor of the house. Taking again for granted that Apte and Godse did see me and had a talk with me, still it was impossible for Badge to have any personal and direct knowledge of what talk they had with me for the simple reason that he could not have either seen or heard, anything happening upstairs on the first floor from the room in which he admits he was sitting on the ground-floor. It would be absurd to take it as a self-evident truth that simply because Apte and Godse went upstairs alone, they must have talked with me about some criminal conspiracy only. Nay, it is far more likely that they could have talked about anything else but the alleged conspiracy.

Especially so because the Prosecution evidence itself proves that on that day Badge, Apte and Godse drove by that very car to a number of persons all over Bombay from one end to the other for quite different objects and had talked on quite different works other than the conspiracy to kill Gandhiji. For example, they went to Afzulpurkar and talked regarding Nizam Civil Resistance movement, and got money as the prosecution witness Afzulpurkar has deposed. They went to the owner of the Dyeing Works Seth Charandas Meghaji whom Apte met alone and yet spoke with him about the Nizam State only and got money, for Nizam State Resistance.[26] They went in-between to Kurla and saw

Patwardhan, Patankar, Kale, etc. etc.[27] talked with them and got money in connection, with the 'Daily Agrani' and 'Hindu Rashtra Prakashan' and so on. It is thus far more likely that Apte and Godse might have met Savarkar, if they met him at all and talked to him upstairs about Hyderabad, Civil Resistance or the 'Daily Agrani' or any other Hindu Sabha work or only enquired about his health and returned. They had talked with all others that whole day long regarding these topics alone and nothing about any conspiracy as is proved by the Prosecution evidence itself.

Thirdly, the same reason disproves Badge's allegation, wherein he says, 'Within 5 or 10 minutes only, Apte, and Godse returned downstairs. They were immediately followed by Savarkar. Savarkar said to Godse and Apte "be successful and come back". *Even if it is assumed that I said this sentence it might have referred to any objects and works referred to above such as the Nizam Civil Resistance,* the raising of funds for the daily paper. 'Agrani' or the sale of the shares of Hindu Rashtra Prakashan Ltd. Company in which I was financially interested or any other legitimate undertaking. As Badge knew nothing as to what talk Apte and Godse had with me upstairs, he could not assert as to what subject my remark 'Be successful etc.' referred.

Fourthly, the sentence which Badge alleges that Apte told him while driving to other houses after leaving my house to the effect that I told Apte that 'Gandhiji's hundred years were over' – is a hearsay and no evidence against us. For, Apte told Badge, what I was alleged to have told Apte. Badge did not hear me personally saying this sentence to Apte. Apte might have told a lie that I said so to Apte. There is nothing to prove and corroborate that I really said so to Apte.

So, whether Badge has lied or Godse and Apte have lied to exploit the moral influence which my name exercised on people to further their alleged criminal conspiracy, in either case it cannot incriminate me in the absence of any independent direct, and material proof to connect me with the criminal knowledge of or participation in that conspiracy.

Fifthly, and above all, both Godse and Apte, positively deny that they ever spoke these sentences to Badge. Apte and Godse moreover deny this whole incident which Badge alleges to have taken place on $17^{th}$ January 1948 and state that they never drove with Badge or others on that day to Savarkar Sadan and never visited Savarkar himself. This contradiction on Apte and Godse's part of the whole story as told by Badge, cuts the very ground from under Badge's allegations.

Sixthly, Badge alleges that on the occasion of this above visit to Savarkar Sadan he with Apte and Godse had hired the taxi belonging to Kotian as a driver. This taxi driver Kotian says in his deposition 'At Shivaji Park I stopped with the taxi. The four passengers got down. So far as I could see they went upto the second house from the corner of the road on my right. They came back to the taxi in about five minutes time'. Now if this taxi driver was brought to corroborate Badge's story, then so far as this incident relating to me is concerned he fails to do it. The taxi driver does not exactly locate my house, he does not know its name, he does not say a word as to whom his passengers wanted to visit in the house, he does not positively mention that it was precisely the second house but only vaguely says that 'As far as I could see from the distance at which I stopped it was the second house up the road on my right hand'. He only says he saw them going only upto the house. He does not say that he saw them entering the house. Thus, his evidence fails to corroborate Badge's allegations regarding his visit to my house, and other details. . . .

Savarkar argued that

if Badge had really any such extraordinary and reckless reverence for my alleged order as to make him risk his very

> life and straightaway start for Delhi on such a dangerous mission, how was it that he precipitately ran away without fulfilling his promise to attack Gandhiji from the front, why he concealed himself and fled away and as he admits had thenceforth 'the only thought of saving himself'?

He attacked Badge personally as one devoid of credibility and even poured scorn on the Prosecution evidence on Godse and Apte's devotion to him in these words, 'Many criminals cherish high respect to the Gurus and guides of their religious sects and profess to follow their tenets. But could ever the complicity of the Guru or guide in the crimes those of his followers be inferred and held proved only on the ground of the professions of loyalty and respect to their Gurus of those criminals?'

*These quotes provide a good flavour of Savarkar's defence and a good glimpse of his personality.* Savarkar battered his own damaged credibility by this assertion:

> It is absolutely relevant if I try to bring to the notice of Your Honour the personal feelings I cherished regarding Gandhiji and Panditji too. I shall not refer to my relations personal and public with Gandhiji in the rather remote past by reciting how in 1908 Gandhiji resided in 'India House' in London owned by the well-known personality, Pandit Shyamji Krishna Varma, and placed under my management and led by me, how Gandhiji and myself lived together as friends and worked together as compatriots, how later on he paid a personal visit with his wife to me and my family and spent hours in happy talks about our old comradeship and current politics. I would not waste the time of the Court in telling how Gandhiji wrote now and then kind notes about me in 'Young India' too. Because those memories would naturally be held as too distant in so far as this case is concerned. Enough to say that inspite of fundamental differences in our ideologies, on some points and in virtue of close affinity on others, there ever continued a mutual

> respect for and a personal goodwill to each other.

Significantly he did not issue a statement denouncing Madanlal's attack on January 20. He had condemned the attempt on Jinnah's life in 1944.

### The judgement

In his Judgement, Judge Atma Charan meticulously analysed Badge's testimony on oath.[28] It is appropriate that his observations on the point in chapter XXIV should be quoted *in extensor.*

> It is now practically a rule of law that an approver must be corroborated both as to the *corpus delicti* and as to the identity of the accused, though corroboration need not be on all the details of the crime nor is it necessary that the corroborative evidence should itself be sufficient for conviction. The nature and the extent of the corroboration required depends upon and varies with the circumstances of each case, particularly the nature of the offence charged, the character and the antecedents of the approver and the degree of suspicion attaching to the evidence, the circumstances in which the approver makes his statement and his motive to implicate the accused falsely.
>
> The examination and the cross-examination of the approver went on from 20.7.1948 till 30.7.1948. He was cross-examined for nearly seven days. There was thus an ample opportunity to observe his demeanour and the manner of his giving evidence. *He gave his version of the facts in a direct and straightforward manner. He did not evade cross-examination or attempt to evade or fence with any question. It would not have been possible for anyone to have given evidence so unfalteringly stretching over such a long period and with such particularity in regard to the facts which had never taken place.* It is difficult to conceive of anyone memorizing so long and so detailed a story if altogether without foundation.
>
> The evidence of the approver may conveniently be

divided into three groups – firstly, the evidence that stands fully corroborated, secondly, the evidence that stands generally corroborated, and thirdly, the evidence that does not stand corroborated in regard to the identity of certain accused.

The approver's evidence that stands fully corroborated has already been discussed earlier. Now I take up the approver's evidence that stands generally corroborated. The approver in his evidence says that he dealt in arms, ammunition and explosives at the time and that Vishnu R. Karkare and Madanlal K. Pahwa along with two more individuals came to inspect the explosives at his house on 9.1.1948. He was called to the Hindu Rashtra Office on 10.1.1948, when he agreed to supply Nathuram V. Godse and Narayan D. Apte with two gun-cotton-slabs and five hand grenades at the Hindu Mahasabha Office at Dadar on 14.1.1948.

It has been argued on behalf of the defence that the individuals who are said to have accompanied Vishnu R. Karkare and Madanlal K. Pahwa to the house of the approver on 9.1.1948 could at least have been produced in corroboration of the approver's story. The evidence produced on behalf of the prosecution goes to show that every effort was made to trace them but they could not be traced. Even if they had appeared as witnesses it is doubtful if their evidence would have amounted to more than that of accomplices.

The approver in his evidence says that he was asked by Narayan D. Apte in the compound of the temple of Dixitji Maharaj also to proceed along with them to Delhi as it had been decided that Mahatma Gandhi be 'finished'. He agreed to do so. He along with Shankar Kistayya proceeded to Delhi and stayed in the Hindu Mahasabha Bhawan along with Madanlal K. Pahwa and Gopal V. Godse from 19.1.1948 till 20.1.1948.

It has been argued on behalf of the defence that at least someone should have been produced from the Hindu

Mahasabha Bhawan in corroboration of the approver's story. The prosecution could have produced no such person in evidence in view of their allegations against the Hindu Mahasabha.

The approver in his evidence says that Narayan D. Apte took him along with Shankar Kistayya on 20.1.1948 to the Birla House and showed him the prayer-platform, the window with trellis-work behind it and the servants-quarters.

It has been argued on behalf of the defence that at least the gate-keeper and some servant living in the quarters should have been produced in corroboration of the approver's story. It is just possible that the gate-keeper and the servants living in the quarters might not have taken any serious notes of the visit of these persons that day to the Birla House. However, it quite stands to reason that Narayan D. Apte would have shown the prayer-platform and the surrounding locality to the approver before proceeding for the intended object to that place. He could not have just asked the approver to enter the room unless he had explained to him first how the matter stood and what was intended to be done there.

The approver in his evidence says that in the Marina Hotel on 20.1.1948 they fixed primers to the gun-cotton-slabs and detonators to the hand-grenades, discussed the plan and distributed the 'stuff' among them. Of course, no direct corroborative evidence to the effect could possibly have been produced on behalf of the prosecution. However, there is an illuminating piece of indirect corroborative evidence to the effect on behalf of the prosecution. The evidence of Nain Singh as supported by Exs. P/17 and P/24 goes to show that three extra teas had been ordered and supplied that day in Room No. 40.

It is a well-known principle in the estimation of evidence that the earlier events may be construed in the light of the subsequent ones. *The approver's story as given above fits in fully with the events that took place subsequently and stands corroborated otherwise by independent evidence.* There is thus no reason as to why reliance be not placed on the approver's evidence that stands generally corroborated.

Now I take up the approver's evidence that does not stand corroborated in regard to the identity of a certain accused – Vinayak D. Savarkar.

The approver in this evidence says that on 14.1.1948 Nathuram V. Godse and Narayan D. Apte took him from the Hindu Mahasabha Office at Dadar to the Savarkar Sadan saying that arrangements will have to be made for keeping the 'stuff'. He had the bag containing the 'stuff' with him, Nathuram V. Godse and Narayan D. Apte then went inside leaving him standing outside the Savarkar Sadan. Nathuram V. Godse and Narayan D. Apte came back 5–10 minutes later with bag containing the 'stuff'.

The approver then says that on 15.1.1948 in the compound of the temple of Dixitji Maharaj Narayan D. Apte told him that Tatyarao Savarkar had decided that Gandhiji should be 'finished' and had entrusted that work to them. The approver then says that on 17.1.1948 Nathuram V. Godse suggested that they should all go and take the last 'darshan' of Tatyarao Savarkar. They then proceeded to the Savarkar Sadan. Narayan D. Apte asked him to wait in the room on the ground floor. Nathuram V. Godse and Narayan D. Apte went up to the first floor and came down after 5–10 minutes. They were followed immediately by Tatyarao Savarkar. Tatyarao Savarkar addressed Nathuram V. Godse and Narayan D. Apte 'yashasvi houn ya' (be successful and come).

Narayan D. Apte on their way back from Savarkar Sadan said that Tatyarao Savarkar had predicted 'tatyarao yani ase bhavishya kele ahe ki gandhijichi sambhar varshe bharali – ata apale kam nischita honar yat kahi sansaya nahi (Gandhiji's hundred years were over – there was no doubt that their work would be successfully finished).

The prosecution case against Vinayak D. Savarkar appears to rest just on the evidence of the approver and the approver alone. The contention on behalf of the prosecution is that part of the approver's story as against Vinayak D. Savarkar to certain extent stands corroborated by the evidence of Miss Shantabai B. Modak and Aitappa K. Kotian.

No doubt there is the evidence of Miss Shantabai B. Modak that Nathuram V. Godse and Narayan D. Apte got down in front of Savarkar Sadan on 14.1.1948. The evidence to the effect, however, in no way goes to establish that Nathuram V. Godse and Narayan D. Apte had got down in front of the Savarkar Sadan to visit Vinayak D. Savarkar. The evidence on record of the case goes to show that not only Vinayak D. Savarkar but A.S. Bhide and Gajanan Damle also reside in the Savarkar Sadan. No doubt there is also the evidence of Aitappa K. Kotian that Nathuram V. Godse, Narayan D. Apte and the approver got down at the Shivaji Park on 17.1.1948.

The evidence to the effect, however, is no corroboration of the approver's story in regard to what the approver says he heard Vinayak D. Savarkar addressing Nathuram V. Godse and Narayan D. Apte. The approver in his evidence says that he had just heard Vinayak D. Savarkar addressing Nathuram V. Godse and Narayan D. Apte 'yashavi houn ya'.

There is nothing on the record of the case to show as to what conversation had taken place just prior to that on the first-floor between Nathuram V. Godse and Narayan D. Apte on the one hand and Vinayak D. Savarkar on the other. There is thus no reason to suppose that the remarks said to have been addressed by Vinayak D. Savarkar to Nathuram V. Godse and Narayan D. Apte in the presence of the approver was in reference to the assassination plot against the life of Mahatma Gandhi.

It would thus be *unsafe* to base any conclusions on the approver's story given above as against Vinayak D. Savarkar.

### Savarkar damned

Given the state of the evidence, the Judge's analysis was fair. It was, he felt, '*unsafe*' to convict Savarkar on Badge's uncorroborated evidence even though he had found him to be a truthful witness. However, his observations in the next Chapter (XXV), only seven pages later, dealing with individual culpability, contradict his own findings on Badge's unchallenged credibility. As it stood, his evidence damned Savarkar totally, only it was 'unsafe' to send him to prison in view of the law of evidence. Yet, while dealing with Savarkar's role the Judge said:

> Vinayak D. Savarkar in his statement says that he had no hand in the 'conspiracy' if any, and had no control whatsoever over Nathuram V. Godse and Narayan D. Apte. It has been mentioned above that the prosecution case against Vinayak D. Savarkar rests just on the evidence of the approver and the approver alone. It has further been mentioned earlier that it would be *unsafe* to base any conclusions on the evidence of the approver as against Vinayak D. Savarkar. *There is thus no reason to suppose that Vinayak D. Savarkar had any hand in what took place at Delhi on 20.1.1948 and 30.1.1948.*

In fact, however, in this case, the conclusion does not follow from the premises.

The last sentence, italicized here, is pure *obiter*. Badge's testimony showed that Savarkar very much had 'a hand in what took place at Delhi' on January 20 and January 30, 1948. It did not suffer from lack of credibility, but from lack of corroboration. The *obiter* was uncalled for and contradicted the Judge's own findings on Badge's credibility.

It is relevant to mention here an incident which took place when Morarji Desai gave evidence. *The Times of India* of September 1, 1948 carried the text of the Chief Prosecutive Counsel, C.K.

Daphtary's application to Judge Atma Charan the previous day. The portion concerning Savarkar read thus,

> In cross-examination of the Honourable Mr Morarji Desai, Counsel for accused number seven [V.D. Savarkar] asked the following question, 'Did you have any other information about Savarkar, besides Professor Jain's statement for directing steps to be taken as regards him?'
>
> Witness answered the question as follows: 'Shall I give the full facts? I am prepared to answer. It is for him [Savarkar] to decide.' Council for accused number seven thereafter stated that he dropped the question. The prosecution submitted that the question answer and the statement of counsel should be recorded but Your Honour declined to do so. It is submitted that the question, the answer and the statement of counsel for accused number seven should have gone on the record.

*Only a year or two after Savarkar's death, his aides spoke up before the Kapur Commission and provided ample corroboration of Badge's evidence.* The Commission's Report notes:

> The statement of Appa Ramchandra Kasar, Bodyguard of V.D. Savarkar which was recorded by the Bombay Police on 4th March, 1948 shows that even in 1946 Apte and Godse were frequent visitors of Savarkar and Karkare also sometimes visited him. . . . In August, 1947 when Savarkar went to Poona in connection with a meeting Godse and Apte were always with Savarkar and were discussing with him the future policy of the Hindu Mahasabha and told them that he himself was getting old and they would have to carry on the work. In the beginning of August, 1947 on the 5th or 6th, there was an All India Hindu convention at Delhi and Savarkar, Godse and Apte travelled together by plane. At the Convention the Congress policies were strongly criticized. On 11th August, Savarkar, Godse and Apte all returned to Bombay together by plane. . . . On or about

13th or 14th January, *Karkare came to Savarkar with a Punjabi youth* and they had an interview with Savarkar for about 15 or 20 minutes. On or about 15th or 16th Apte and Godse had an interview with Savarkar at 9.30 p.m. After about a week or so, may be 23rd or 24th January, Apte and Godse again came to Savarkar and had a talk with him at about 10 or 10.30 a.m. for about half an hour. . . .

Gajanan Vishnu Damle, secretary of Savarkar, was also examined on 4th March, 1948 by the Bombay Police. He said that he had known N.D. Apte of the 'Agrani' for the last four years. Apte started a rifle club at Ahmednagar and also was an Honorary Recruiting Officer during the war. Apte was frequent visitor to Savarkar's house and sometimes came with Godse. Savarkar had lent Rs 15000 to Apte and Godse for the newspaper when security was demanded from the Agrani. That paper was stopped and the newpaper called the Hindu Rashtra was started. Savarkar was one of its Directors and Apte and Godse were the Managing Agents. He knew V.R. Karkare who was a Hindu Mahasabha worker at Ahmednagar for about three years and occasionally visited Savarkar. Badge was also known to him for the last three years. He also used to visit Savarkar.

In the first week of January 1948, Karkare and a Punjabi refugee boy came to see Savarkar and they both had an interview with Savarkar for about half an hour or 45 minutes. Neither of them came to see Savarkar again. Apte and Godse came to see Savarkar about the middle of January 1948, late at night. The statements of both these witnesses show that both Apte and Godse were frequent visitors of Savarkar at Bombay and at Conferences and at every meeting they are shown to have been with Savarkar. . . . This evidence also shows that Karkare was also well known to Savarkar and was also a frequent visitor. Badge also used to visit Savarkar. Dr Parchure also visited him. *All this shows that people who were subsequently involved in the murder of Mahatma Gandhi were all congregating sometime or the other at Savarkar Sadan and sometimes had long interviews with Savarkar.*

> *It is significant that Karkare and Madanlal visited Savarkar before they left for Delhi and Apte and Godse visited him both before the bomb was thrown and also before the murder was committed and on each occasion they had long interviews.*
>
> It is specially to be noticed that Godse and Apte were with him at public meetings held at various places in the years 1946, 1947 and 1948.

Had they but testified in Court, Savarkar would have been convicted. There was none of the ambiguity surrounding Godse and Apte's visits to Savarkar on January 14 and 17, 1948. A.R. Kasar, Savarkar's bodyguard, told the Kapur Commission that they visited him on or about he 23rd or 24th January which was when they returned from Delhi *after* the bomb incident. G.V. Damle, Savarkar's secretary, deposed that Godse and Apte saw Savarkar 'in the middle of January and sat with him [Savarkar] in his garden'.[29]

Justice Kapur's findings however are all too clear. After listing the information available to Nagarvala he concluded: 'All these facts taken together were destructive of any theory other than the conspiracy to murder by Savarkar and his group.' Nagarvala tripped because he chased the theory, based on wrong information, that the group wished only to kidnap Gandhi.[30]

In his Crime Report No. 1, Nagarvala had stated that 'Savarkar was at the back of the conspiracy and that he was feigning illness'.[31] Nagarvala's letter of January 31, 1948, the day after the assassination, mentioned that Savarkar, Godse and Apte met for 40 minutes 'on the eve of their departure to Delhi' on the strength of what Kasar and Damle disclosed to him. 'These two had access to the house of Savarkar without any restriction'.[32] *In short, Godse and Apte met Savarkar again, in the absence of Badge and in addition to their meetings on January 14 and 17.*

Now for the Mahasabha-RSS nexus. Morarji Desai testified that they 'were working together'.[33] Justice Kapur found that 'many RSS members were members of the Hindu Mahasabha'.[34] One of his conclusions read, '(4) (a) The RSS was the best organized and militant Hindu organization India and although it was not affiliated to the Hindu Mahasabha, its prominent organizers and workers were members or sponsors of the Hindu Mahasabha ideology'.[35]

Why was the Kapur Commission set up? For nearly the same reasons which prompted the establishment of the Chandrachud Commission on Deen Dayal Upadhyaya's murder in the wake of the acquittal of the two accused. After Gopal Godse's release from prison, a meeting was held to felicitate him in Poona on November 11, 1964. Speaking on the occasion, G.V. Ketkar, former editor of *Kesari*, claimed that Nathuram Godse used to discuss with him the pros and cons of his plans to murder Gandhi. After the bomb explosion on January 20, Badge told him of 'their future plans'. Predictably, this caused a furore in Parliament and in the press. On March 22, 1965 a Commission of Inquiry was set up, broadly, to ascertain whether Ketkar or any one else had prior information of the crime, whether it was communicated to the Government and, if so, what was the action taken. The Commission had before it a mass of material which is not available to a court of law and was not submitted to Judge Atma Charan.

Justice Chandrachud described the difference between the scope of a criminal trial and an inquiry most ably in his Report.

> The scope of this inquiry is wider than the scope of the Sessions Trial. I must determine why the murder was committed – a question that has wider ramifications than the question before the Sessions Court, namely, whether the accused before it were guilty of the crime imputed to them. . . . Any further inquiry was uncalled for. That is why the learned Judge observed that '*a criminal trial is not a probe or inquiry into the truth about occurrence*'. My inquiry is what a criminal trial cannot be – *I can conduct a probe into the real truth.*[36]

Justice Jivan Lal Kapur found 'the real truth' which Judge Atma Charan could not. In doing so, he laid bare the pattern underlying earlier crimes – Curzon Wylie's murder in 1909, Jackson's murder in 1909, an attempt to murder Hotson in 1931, and Gandhi's murder in 1948. Collins and Lapierre write: 'The Andaman Islands, however, had taught Savarkar a lesson. He concealed his connection with the killers so carefully that the police were never able to build a case against him.'[37] They characterized him as 'the zealot whose unseen hands had controlled the flow of at least three political assassinations.'[38]

In 1948, Savarkar escaped the clutches of law. In 1969, Justice Kapur vindicated Vallabhbhai Patel. If, following a long established pattern, Savarkar managed to conceal his own role in the murder, shortly after the Gandhi murder trial, faced with incarceration and personal loss, Savarkar yet again preferred to tender a grovelling apology and write a demeaning undertaking. This, again, is a pattern in his life that begins in 1911 and goes all the way to 1950.

# 6 THE AFTERMATH

THE AFTERMATH OF Gandhi's assassination is still very much with us.

The Babri Masjid was demolished by Savarkar's followers on December 6, 1992, as part of the crusade for Hindutva. That crime has been widely compared to that of the Mahatma's assassination. Both draw from the Sangh *parivar* only mused expressions of regret, never denunciation. On February 10, 1948, shortly after the murder, Nehru wrote to Maherchand Mahajan, Prime Minister of Jammu and Kashmir: 'I have learnt that in Jammu there was a hartal because of Savarkar's arrest. I am sorry to learn this because it denotes a certain sympathy with those who are supposed to be associated with Gandhiji's assassination'.[1] Vallabhbhai Patel reminded Savarkar's acolyte Shyama Prasad Mookerjee, on May 6, 1948 when he tried to defend Savarkar and the Hindu Mahasabha, that while the organization as such was not concerned, 'but at the same time, we cannot shut our eyes to the fact that *an appreciable number* of the members of the Mahasabha gloated over the tragedy and distributed sweets. On this matter, reliable reports have come to us from all parts of the country'.[2]

There has been much discussion in recent times about the outrageous rewriting of history that is taking place at the instance of the RSS. A reputed international newspaper reports:

> The Hindu nationalists frequently take up the theme of 'invasions by Muslim rulers' during the medieval era. But *one of the most glaring omissions is the assassination of Mohandas K. Gandhi, regarded as the father of the nation.* The event is not

> mentioned at all in the new history books. Gandhi was assassinated a few months after Independence in 1947 by a Hindu fanatic who believed that Gandhi's policies appeased the nation's Muslims. The gunman, it was later found out, had once belonged to a militaristic Hindu brotherhood that spawned the ruling BJP.[3]

Advani and Vajpayee are today asking the country to acclaim Savarkar as a national hero. Savarkar escaped conviction in the Special Court presided over by a District and Sessions Judge, but he received his desserts at the hands of a former Judge of the Supreme Court who had a background of nationalist commitment before Independence. After his release, Savarkar went his way demonstrating the lack of character which had marked his life right till his death in 1966. But Savarkarism flourishes still and is being propagated by men in the highest seats of power – Prime Minister Vajpayee, and Deputy Prime Minister Advani. The Chief Minister of Gujarat, Narendra Modi, has demonstrated his commitment to Hindutva in the despicable manner that comes naturally to him. *It is this phenomenon, the celebration of Hindutva, that should prod serious reflection.*

### The 1950 undertaking

During the emergency the RSS supremo, M.D. Deoras, wrote cringing letters to Prime Minister Indira Gandhi, Chief Minister of Maharashtra S.B. Chavan, and Vinoba Bhave.[4] Here too he was following in the hallowed tradition set by V.D. Savarkar. The last in the ignoble series of his demeaning assurances was offered as late as in 1950. The episode is dutifully recounted by his Boswell, Dhananjay Keer.

It occurred in the context of the Nehru-Liaqat pact on the minorities. Savarkar, along with other Mahasabha leaders, was detained on April 4, 1950 under the Preventive Detention Act, 1950. He wrote to the State Government on April 26, 1950 pleading for his release from prison. Keer records, 'but in case Government was not inclined to grant the request for unconditional release, Savarkar urged that he should be released *under the condition* that he would not take part in current politics *for any period Government might lay down*. . . . Savarkar added that it was a matter of public knowledge that he had been already contemplating to retire shortly from the political field'.[5]

The Government of Bombay rejected Savarkar's offer. His son Vishwas filed a habeas corpus application in the Bombay High Court. When it came up for hearing before the Chief Justice M.C. Chagla and Justice P.B. Gajendragadkar, the Advocate General, C.K. Daphtary, asked for a day's time to take instructions from the Government. On July 13, he informed the court that

> he was authorized to state that if Savarkar would give an undertaking that he would not participate in political activities and would remain at his own house in Bombay, Government would agree to his release. Their Lordship made the order of release on July 13 on an undertaking given by K.N. Dharap, who appeared on behalf of Savarkar, that Savarkar would not take any part whatever in political activity and would remain in his house in Bombay. This undertaking was to last a period of one year or upto the next general elections in India or in case of India being involved in any war, whichever event took place first.[6]

Savarkar said on July 20, 1950 that 'in view of the restrictions imposed on me by Government . . . preventing me from taking part in politics for a specified period, I must inevitably resign even the primary membership of the Hindu Mahasabha'.[7]

After his release Savarkar moved closer to the RSS. On July 15, 1949 he wired to the RSS supremo, M.S. Golwalkar: 'Hearty felicitations on your release. Long live the Sangh as the valorous champion of Hindudom.'[8] Savarkar's wishes have come true. The RSS has lived a long life – too long, many feel. The Hindu Mahasabha, on the other hand, has declined rapidly. Savarkar died a broken man. It was little consolation to Savarkar that, on his 80th birthday, the RSS chief M.S. Golwalkar acknowledged in a speech on May 15, 1963, his debt to *Hindutva* written forty years earlier.[9] He knew that he had long ceased to be a player. The tide had turned against him much earlier. In fact, when he returned to India in the twenties any hopes he had of being acclaimed as the saviour had evaporated. India had already given its heart and mind to another suitor – Gandhi. Hence Savarkar's bitterness for the man. This is a neglected aspect of his personality which Robert Payne noted with remarkable perception: 'Long before he died, he knew that he had been the man waiting in the wings for the call to occupy the centre of the stage, but the call never came.'[10]

### Godse and RSS

Savarkar moved closer to the RSS after the Gandhi murder. But what about Gandhi's assassin, Nathuram Godse? What were his links with the RSS? Here is what Advani had to say on the question: 'Nathuram Godse was a bitter critic of the Rashtriya Swayamsevak Sangh. His charge was that the RSS had made Hindus impotent. *We have had nothing to do with Godse.* The Congress is in the habit of reviving this allegation against us when it finds nothing else'.[11]

Nathuram Godse's brother Gopal nailed these denials to the counter in a devastating interview:

> *Q.* Were you a part of the RSS?
> *A.* All the brothers were in the RSS. Nathuram, Dattatreya, myself and Govind. You can say we grew up in the RSS rather than in our homes. It was like a family to us.
> *Q.* Nathuram stayed in the RSS? He did not leave it?
> *A.* Nathuram had become a *baudhik karyavah* (intellectual worker) in the RSS. *He said in his statement that he left the RSS. He said it because Golwalkar and the RSS were in a lot of trouble after the murder of Gandhi. But he did not leave the RSS.*
> *Q.* Advani has recently said that Nathuram had nothing to do with RSS.
> *A.* I have countered him, saying it is *cowardice to say that.* You can say that RSS did not pass a resolution, saying that, 'go and assassinate Gandhi.' *But you do not disown him* [Nathuram]. The Hindu Mahasabha did not disown him.

> In 1944 Nathuram started doing Hindu Mahasabha work when he had been a *baudhik karyavah* in the RSS.[12]

The Sangh *parivar* will never be able to live down its murky past. Savarkar's *Hindutva* cannot be separated either from his advocacy of repression or from his advocacy of violence. The Godse connection is the mark of Cain which Savarkarism will ever bear on its person.

The BJP's studied revival of the Savarkar cult in word and conduct reveals that it is out to make a determined bid to recast the Indian polity on the basis of Hindutva. That will not come to pass. The nation's reaction to the Gujarat pogrom of 2002 reveals where its heart lies.

# APPENDICES: SAVARKAR'S APOLOGIES AND ASSURANCES TO THE GOVERNMENT, 1911–1950

## Appendix 1: 1911, 1913

Savarkar arrived in the Andamans in June, 1911. Before the year was out, he submitted to the Government of India a 'petition for clemency'. The text of this petition, however, is not available. Savarkar referred to it in his next petition sent on November 14, 1913. The bulk of the letter concerned facilities in jail and a request for transfer to an 'Indian Jail for there I would earn (a) remission; (b) would have a visit from my people . . . .'

The last and the revealing paragraph of the petition is set out below:

> In the end may I remind your honour to be so good as to go through the petition for clemency, that I had sent in 1911, and to sanction it for being forwarded to the Indian Government? The latest development of the Indian Politics and the conciliating policy of the Government have thrown open the constitutional line once more. Now no man having the good of India and Humanity at Heart will blindly step on the thorny paths which in the excited and hopeless situation of India in 1906–1907 beguiled us from the path of peace and progress. Therefore if the Government in their manifold beneficence and merely release me I for one cannot but be the staunchest advocate of constitutional progress and loyalty to the English Government which is the foremost condition of that progress. As long as we are

in jails, there cannot be real happiness and joy in hundreds and thousands of homes of His Majesty's loyal subjects in India, for blood is thicker than water; but if we be released the people will instinctively raise a shout of joy and gratitude to the Government, who knows how to forgive and correct, more than how to chastise and avenge. Moreover my conversation to the constitutional line would bring back all those misled young men in India and abroad who were once looking up to me as their guide, I am ready to serve the Government in any capacity they like, for as my conversion is conscientious so I hope my future conduct would be. By keeping me in jail nothing can be got in comparison to what would be otherwise. The Mighty alone can afford to be merciful and therefore where else can the prodigal son return but to the parental doors of the Government? Hoping your Honour will kindly take into notion these points.

## Appendix 2: 1924, 1925

Documents published in *Frontline*, April 7, 1995.

With compliments from the Director of Information of Bombay. P. 2/5-1-24.

The Government of Bombay have decided on the release of Vinayak Damodar Savarkar and the following government resolution has been issued by the Home Department.

1. 'In exercise of the power conferred by Section 401 of the Code of Criminal Procedure, 1898, the Governor in Council hereby remits conditionally the unexpired portion of the sentences of transportation for life passed upon Vinayak Damodar Savarkar.

2. 'The order for the conditional release for the convict should be sent to the Supritendent, Yeravada Central Prison, who should take an agreement from the convict accepting the conditions specified in the order, and forward it to the Government, through the Inspector General of Prisons, with the report that the convict has been released in pursuance of the Order.'

The conditions attached to the release of releases are these:

(1) 'That the said Vinayak Damodar Savarkar will reside within the territories administered by the Governor of Bombay in Council and within the Ratnagiri District within the said territories, and will not go beyond the limits of that district without the permission of the Government, or in case of urgency of the District Magistrate.

(2) 'That he will not engage publicly or privately in any manner of political activities without the consent of the Government for a period of five years, such restriction being renewable at the discretion of Government at the expiry of the said term.'

Mr Savarkar has already indicated his – acceptance of these

terms. He has also, thought it was explained to him that it was in no way made condition of his release, submitted the following statement: – 'I hereby acknowledge that I had a fair trial and just sentence. I heartily abhor – methods of violence resorted to in days gone by, and I feel myself duty bound to uphold Law and the constitution to the best of my powers and am willing to make the Reform a success in so far as I may be allowed to do in future.'

True Copy,

For Suprintendent.

* * *

Shirgaon, 9$^{th}$ May 1925.

To
D. O'Flynn, Esquire,
Acting Deputy Secretary to the Government of
Bombay, Home Department.

Sir,
I have received yesterday your letter dated 6$^{th}$ May regarding the article in the 'Maratha' on the subject of the riots at Kohat.

This letter makes me revise the meaning I put on the terms of my conditions which to my mind meant refraining from discussing or dealing with any question of current policies i.e. any matter that refer to the nature of activity of the Government *directly* bearing on its political aspect internal or international. In the light of this interpretation I had honestly striven to guide my public activities. But this order had forced me to understand the condition in a narrower sense.

While I am trying to define to myself my position in view of this new order I most humbly beg to request in as much as this order came to my hand on the 8$^{th}$ of May, all my writings and speeches prior to that date should be subjected to that interpretation as they were guided by the first and direct interpretation I naturally put on the meaning of terms of my conditions of release. Of course all my actions subsequent to the date of the receipt of your letter would be subjected to this interpretation.

I have the honour to be,

Sir,

Your most obedient servant,

Sd. V.D. Savarkar.

True Copy.

* * *

Extract from an article in *Frontline*, dated April 7, 1995:

In February 1925, serious communal trouble broke out in Kohat town of the North-West Frontier Province (NWFP). Jivan Das of Kohat had written a booklet, *Rangila Rasool*, portraying Prophet Mohammed in bad light. This caused communal riots in Kohat, in the other town in the NWFP and in the western parts of then Punjab. As rumours spread throughout the country, Savarkar felt so agitated he wrote an article in the *Mahratta* of Pune on March 1, 1925.

The Government did not take to this kindly. He was warned that 'any future writings of a similar character will be regarded by Government a sufficient justification for reconsidering the question of his release'. Post-haste, despite his having very strong views on the Kohat incidents, Savarkar sent a longish explanation at the end of which he thanked the Government for having given him an opportunity to explain himself and hoped that in future too they would be pleased to be as kindly disposed towards him. In this letter, dated April 6, he made it clear he would have no truck with the idea of Swaraj: 'The only place where the word Swaraj occurs is at the end of the third paragraph and there it is obvious that a reference is not at all to show or indicate what I or other people think of Swaraj but in what exaggerated terms Mr Gandhi thinks of Khilafat.'

The Government was not mollified even by this. It told him curtly on May 6, 1925 it considered his explanation far from satisfactory: ' . . . it should have been obvious to you that an article of the nature which you published in the issue of *Mahratta* of the 1st March, 1925 was bound to inflame the feelings and increase the tension between Hindus and Muhammadans and was contrary to your undertaking not to engage in any manner in political activities without the consent of Government.'

This letter was received by Savarkar on May 8 through the District Magistrate. It so unnerved him that the very next day he wrote back to D. O'Flynn, Acting Deputy Secretary to the Government of Bombay, Home Department, thus: ' . . . I most Humbly beg to request in as much as this order came to my had on the 8th of May, all my writings and speeches prior to that date should not be subjected to that interpretation as they were guided by the first or direct interpretation I naturally put on the meaning of terms of my conditions of release.'

Savarkar took fright that the Government might resort to some severe action against him for some of the writings and speeches made between March and May 8. One warning from the Government, and his concern for the so-called welfare of Hindus had disappeared into thin air.

## Appendix 3: 1948

Arthur Road Prison,
Bombay.

Dated 22-2-1948

To
The Commissioner of Police,
Bombay.

Sir,

Your notice No. 1202 of 1948 was served on me day before yesterday.

(I) My submission to the charges is that I never promoted hatred and incited Hindus to hate or to commit acts of violence against the Mohammedans as Mohammedans. I have been an advocate throughout my life of Genuine Indian Nationalism. I always emphasized that all citizens who owned loyalty to the Indian State must be loved as fellow citizens and treated with equality of rights and obligations to the state irrespective of caste, creed or religion, without the least distinction being made as Hindu or a Mohammedan or a Parsee or a Jew. 'One man one vote' and 'services to go by merit alone' these two principles will be found endlessly repeated in all my writings and speeches made throughout my political career for some 50 years in the past.

But it is this admitted fact that I have been exhorting the Hindus to defend themselves in virtue of the logic of self-defence was, I believe, misunderstood or misinterpreted as an incitement to the Hindus to commit violence against all Muslims alike. I submit that this interpretation is wrong and unwarranted. Sardar Patel himself in replying to provoking speeches of some Muslim leaders retorted 'sword shall be met with sword'. But that does not surely mean that he hated all Muslims alike or incited violence.

(II) To substantiate the fact I need not quote one of my latest, statements issued just before my arrest and published in the 'Times' in the course of which after denouncing the gruesome crime of the assassination of Mahatma Gandhi the fratricidal crimes committed by the mob fury, I implored every patriotic citizen to bear in mind that a successful national revolution and a newly-born National State could have no worse enemy than a fratricidal civil war, specially so when it was surrounded from outside by alien hospitality.

(III) In the end I beg to submit that I am now some 65 years old. For the last three years I have been every now and then confined to bed owing to attacks of heart-ache and debility. On the 15th of August last I accepted and raised on my house our new National Flag even to the embarrassment of some of my followers.

Consequently, in order to disarm all suspicion and to back up the above heart representation I wish to express my willingness to give an undertaking to the Government that I shall refrain from taking part in any communal or political public activity for any period the Government may require in case I am released on that condition.

Sd/- V.D. Savarkar

* * *

For Savarkar's undertaking of 1950, see chapter 6, 'The Aftermath'.

# NOTES

## 1 The myth and the man

1 Italics added, throughout. Bisheshwar Mishra, *The Times of India*, May 5, 2002.

2 *The Statesman*, May 5, 2002.

3 Shekhar Iyer, *The Hindustan Times*, May 5, 2002.

4 India Office (IO), MSS EMF 125/8 1939, Letters to the Secretary of State for India, quoted in Marzia Casolari's outstanding paper 'Hindutva's Foreign Tie-up in the 1930's: Archival Evidence', *Economic and Political Weekly*, January 22, 2000, p. 226. It is a documented expose of 'the existence of direct contacts between the representatives of the fascist regime, including Mussolini, and Hindu nationalists. These contacts demonstrate that Hindu nationalism had much more than an abstract interest in the ideology and practice of fascism.'

5 *Hindustan Times*, May 5, 2002.

6 The issue of Gandhi's murder and Savarkar's involvement in it is taken up in greater detail in chapter 5 below.

7 Rudrangshu Mukherjee (ed.,) *The Penguin Gandhi Reader*, Penguin Books, 1993, p. 167.

8 *Constituent Assembly Debates*, volume IV, pp. 737–62.

9 S.S. Savarkar and G.M. Joshi (eds.), *Historic Statements by V.D. Savarkar*, Popular Prakashan, Mumbai 1967, pp. 205–06.

10 *The Statesman*, May 5.

11 *The Organiser*, June 2, 1991.

12 For a full exposition see *Hindu Rashtra Darshan*, a collection of the Presidential Speeches delivered from the Hindu Mahasabha platform by V.D. Savarkar, L.G. Khare, Mumbai, 1949. Hereinafter cited as *HRD*.

13 See A.G. Noorani, *The RSS and the BJP: A Division of Labour*, LeftWord Books, New Delhi, second edition, 2001, p. 62. See pp.

59–66 for a survey of the BJP's transition from 'Gandhian socialism' in 1980 to Hindutva in 1990.

[14] *Debonair*, August 1980.

[15] *The Hindu*, August 16, 2002.

[16] *The Times of India*, April 14, *1981*.

[17] Interestingly, and revealingly, no one in the BJP repudiated its Vice President's remarks.

[18] Editorial, *Organiser*, January 11, 1970. The *Organiser* was then edited by K.R. Malkani, who subsequently became a Vice President of the BJP.

[19] Noorani, *The RSS and the BJP*, p. 51.

[20] *The Times of India*, May 18, 1991.

[21] *Indian Express*, May 21, 1991.

[22] *Sunday Observer*, June 2, 1991.

[23] Editorial, *The Times of India*, May 21, 1991.

[24] *The Times of India*, October 17, 1989.

[25] *The Statesman*, August 11, 2002.

[26] Dhananjay Keer, *Veer Savarkar*, Popular Prakashan, Bomaby, 1966. The first edition of this book was published under the title *Savarkar and His Times* in 1950.

[27] Keer, *Veer Savarkar*, p. 4.

[28] Robert Payne, *The Life and Death of Mahatma Gandhi*, The Bodley Head, 1969, pp. 206–07.

[29] *Terrorism in India 1917–1936*, Government of India Press, Simla, 1937, p. 118.

[30] M.R. Jayakar, *The Story of My Life*, Asia Publishing House, 1958, volume 1, p. 103.

[31] Keer, *Veer Savarkar*, p. 49.

[32] Payne, *Life and Death of Mahatma Gandhi*, pp. 617–18.

[33] Ibid., p. 204.

[34] Keer, *Veer Savarkar*, p. 52.

[35] Jayakar, *The Story of My Life*, p. 116.

[36] Swatantriya Veer Savarkar, *A Guide to the Indian Revolutionary Movement*. The volume contains *The Indian War of Independence 1857*, *Dedication to the Martyrs of 1857* and *Letters from Andamans*. *Samagra Savarkar Wangmaya*, volume V, Maharashtra Prantik Hindusabha, Pune, 1963. Hereinafter cited as *SSW*.

[37] We shall offer a detailed critique of the work in chapter 2 below.

[38] Keer, *Veer Savarkar*, p. 74.

[39] Ibid., pp. 75–87.

[40] P.B. Vachha, *Famous Judges, Lawyers and Cases of Bombay: A Judicial History of Bombay During the British Period*, N.M. Tripathi, Bombay, 1962, pp. 292–95.

[41] R.C. Majumdar, *Penal Settlements in Andamans*, Gazetters Unit,

Department of Culture, Ministry of Education and Social Welfare, Government of India, New Delhi, 1975, pp. 211–13.

42 Keer, *Veer Savarkar*, p. 149.

43 Krishnan Dubey and Venkitesh Ramakrishnan, 'Far from heroism: The tale of "Veer Savarkar"', *Frontline*, April 7, 1995. See Appendix for the texts of all his undertakings available between 1913 and 1950.

44 Keer, *Savarkar and his Times*, p. 180; *Veer Savarkar*, p. 192.

45 Intelligence Bureau, *Terrorism in India (1917–1936)*, p. 121.

46 Payne, *Life and Death of Mahatma Gandhi*, p. 631.

47 Keer, *Veer Savarkar*, 1966, p. 191.

48 K.M. Munshi, *Indian Constitutional Documents*, volume 1, *Pilgrimage to Freedom (1909–1950)*, Bharatiya Vidya Bhawan, 1967, p. 51.

49 Larry Collins and Dominique Lapierre, *Freedom at Midnight*, Vikas, 1976, p. 362.

50 *Report of Commission of Inquiry into Conspiracy to Murder Mahatma Gandhi*, Government of India Press, New Delhi, 1970, volume II, p. 303, para 25.106.

51 Keer, *Veer Savarkar*, pp. 368 and 371.

52 *HRD*, pp. 26 and 64.

53 R.C. Majumdar (General Editor) and A.K. Majumdar (Assistant Editor), *Struggle for Freedom*, Bhartiya Vidya Bhavan, Mumbai, 1969, p. 611.

54 Jayakar, *Story of My Life* volume II, p. 541.

55 B.R. Ambedkar, *Pakistan or Partition of India*, Thacker & Co. Ltd, Bombay, third edition. 1946, p. 130.

56 *The Statesman*, February 26, 2000.

57 See A.G. Noorani, *The Trial of Bhagat Singh: Politics of Justice*, Oxford University Press, 2001.

58 Darga Das (ed.) *Sardar Patel's Correspondence 1945–50*, Navajivan Publishing house, Ahmedabad, 1973, volume 6, p. 63.

59 Ibid., p. 65.

60 Keer, *Veer Savarkar*, p. 369.

61 Darga Das (ed.), *Sardar Patel's Correspondence*, p. 66.

62 *Indian Express*, June 6, 1991.

63 Darga Das (ed.), *Sardar Patel's Correspondence*, p. 321.

64 Ibid., p. 323.

65 Ibid., pp. 56–57.

66 *Report Regarding the Facts and Circumstances Relating to the Death of Shri Deen Dayal Upadhyaya*, Government of India Press, New Delhi, 1970.

67 Ibid., pp. 61–63.

68 Ibid., pp. 120–21.

69 Mushirul Hasan (ed.), *Islam and Indian Nationalism: Reflections on*

*Abul Kalam Azad*, Manohar, 1992, pp. 6–7.

70 See Noorani, *The RSS and the BJP*, p. 8.

71 *Hindu Mahasabha Records, File No. 13,* quoted in Prabha Dixit, *Communalism: A Struggle for Power,* Orient Longman, 1974, pp. 168–69.

72 *Debates of the Legislative Council of Bombay*, volume 14, part 10, column 314.

## 2 Savarkar's nationalism

1 Asoka Mehta, *1857: A Great Rebellion,* Hind Kitabs, Bombay 1946, p. 7. Dedicated to Jayaprakash Narayan, this excellent book was written in prison between 1940–45. Its bibliography testifies to the author's research; his comments to his respect for the historical truth.

2 Ibid., pp. 68–70

3 *The Telegraph,* May 12 and 13, 1988.

4 *SSW*, p. 3. Further references to this text are embedded in the main body of our text.

5 V.D. Savarkar, *Six Glorious Epochs of Indian History*, Rajadhani Granthnagar, New Delhi, 1970. S.T. Godbole translated the Marathi text into English, and it was published by Bal Savarkar, his secretary. It was completed in 1963.

6 Ibid., p. 461.

## 3 Andamans and the origins of Hindutva

1 V.D. Savarkar, *The Story of My Transportation of Life,* English translation of the Marathi text by V.N. Naik, Sadbhakti Publications, Mumbai 1950. See also *An Echo from Andamans,* letters written by V.D. Savarkar to his brother Dr N. Savarkar, Vishwnath Vinayak Kelkar, Mumbai; reproduced in *SSW*. Both these texts are cited here with references to pages as in *SSW*.

2 R.C. Majumdar, *Penal Settlements in Andamans.*

3 *SSW*, p. 481. Subsequent references to *SSW* are contained in our main text.

4 The two volumes in question had been edited by K.N. Panikkar and Sumit Sarkar.

5 John Keegan, *The First World War,* Alfred A. Knopf, New York 1999, p. 191.

6 Expectedly, Gandhi is ridiculed repeatedly in the book. For instance, see pp. 521, 522, 556, 563.

7 Keer, *Savarkar and His Times*, p. 108.

[8] Ibid., pp. 108–09.
[9] R.C. Majumdar, *Penal Settlements*, pp. 201–02; see also notes, p. 234.
[10] Mushirul Hasan, 'Text books and Imagined History: The BJP's Intellectual Agenda', *India International Centre Quarterly*, Summer 2002, pp. 79–80.
[11] R.C. Majumdar, *Penal Settlements*, p. 201.
[12] Ibid., pp. 204–05.
[13] Ibid., p. 232.
[14] Ibid., p. 243.

## 4 Hindutva vs. Hinduism

[1] Bipan Chandra, *Communalism in Modern India*, Vikas, 1984, p. 168.
[2] See the Chapter on Islamic Fundamentalism in A.G.Noorani, *Islam and Jihad*, Leftword Books, New Delhi, 2002, pp. 52–76
[3] Noorani, *The RSS and the BJP*, 2001, pp. 7–8.
[4] See A.G. Noorani, 'Legal Aspects to the Issue', in Sarvepalli Gopal, *Anatomy of a Confrontation: The Babri Masjid–Ram Janmabhoomi Issue*, Viking, 1991, p. 77.
[5] Prabha Dixit, *Communalism: A Struggle for Power*, p. 170.
[6] Ibid., p. 171.
[7] V.D. Savarkar, *Hindutva: Who is a Hindu?* S.S. Savarkar, Publisher Veer Savarkar Prakashan, Mumbai, 5th edition, 1969. All subsequent references to this essay are contained in the main body of the text.
[8] Neena Vyas, *The Hindu*, May 9, 2002.
[9] Noorani, *The RSS and the BJP*, 2001, p. 18
[10] Keer, *Veer Savarkar*, 1966, p. 527.
[11] Golwalkar, *Bunch of Thoughts*, Vikrama Prakashan, Bangalore, 1968.
[12] Ibid., p. 53.
[13] Swapan Dasgupta, 'Nationhood Specified: Hindutva as a Double-Edged Sword', *The Times of India*, June 9, 1993.
[14] *The Hindustan Times*, March 28, 2002.
[15] *The Times of India*, May 7, 2002.
[16] Tapan Raychaudhuri, 'Swami Vivekananda's Construction of Hinduism', in William Radice (ed.), *Swami Vivekanada and the Modernization of Hinduism*, OUP, 1998, p. 16.
[17] Walter K. Andersen and Shridhar D. Damle, *The Brotherhood in Saffron*, Vistaar, New Delhi, 1987, p. 33. See p. 43 on Golwalkar's debt to G.D. Savarkar.
[18] Keer, *Veer Savarkar* p. 175.
[19] See Praveen Swami, *The Kargil War*, LeftWord Books, 2000, p. 97 for Advani's Sindhu Darshan festival at Leh in 1998 and 1999.

20 Dr Ramesh Yashwant Prabhoo vs. Prabhakar K. Kante, 1996, Supreme Court Cases p.130 and Manohar Joshi vs. Nitin Bhawrao Patil and another (1996) ISCC 169. For a detailed critique see *The Supreme Court on Hindutva*, in A.G.Noorani, *Citizens Rights, Judges and State Accountability*, OUP, 2002, pp. 76–83.

21 Dr M. Ismail Faruqui and Others vs. Union of India and Others. (1994) 6SCC 360, See A.G. Noorani, *Citizens's Rights, Judges and State Accountability*, Oxford University Press, 2002, pp. 66–75 for a detailed critique of Justice Verma's performance.

22 Dr Ramesh Prabhoo vs Prabhakar K. Kunte (1996), Supreme Court Cases p. 130 and Manohar Joshi–Nitin B. Patil. Ibid., p. 169.

23 Abhinam Singh vs C.D. Commachen & Ors. (1996) 3 SCC665 at 671.

24 Dr Das Rao Deshmukh vs. Kamal Kishore Nanasaheb & Ors. (1995) 5 S.C.C. 123 at 138.

25 For a detailed critique of Justice Verma's judgement see Noorani, *Citizen's Rights*, pp. 76–85.

26 Golwalkar *Bunch of Thoughts*, p. 134. Subsequent references in the main text.

27 B.B. Mishra, *The Indian Political Parties*, OUP, 1976, pp. 162–63.

28 Andersen and Damle, *Brotherhood in Saffron*, pp. 28–29.

29 Ibid., pp. 43–44. See also Andersen's excellent article, 'The Rastriya Swayam Sewak Sangh', *Economic and Political Weekly*, March 25, 1972, p. 673. Cited hereafter as Andersen, RSS.

30 Cited hereafter as *HRD*. All subsequent references are included in the text.

31 *Indian Express*, September 25, 1989.

32 Sitaramayya, *The History of the Indian National Congress*, Bombay, Padma, 1947, Vol. II 1935–1947, pp 513–514.

33 This, and the following quotation, are from Shyama Prasad Mookerjee, *Leaves from a Diary*, Oxford University Press 1993, pp. 175–90.

34 Ibid.

35 Ibid., p. 106.

36 Joya Chaterji, *Bengal Divided, Hindu Communalism and Partition*, Cambridge University Press, 1995, p. 189. A footnote shows that this was drawn from an undated note by Mookerjee himself.

37 'Hindutva's Foreign Tie-up in the 1930's, Archival Evidence', *Economic & Political Weekly*, January 22, 2000, pp. 218–28.

38 Casolari's source is NAI, Home Poll Department, August 28, 1942, intelligence report 'Rashtriya Swayam Sewak Sangh', dated March 7, 1942.

39 Casolari's sources are MSA, Home Special Dept 60 D (g) Pt. II,

1937. Extract from the Bombay Secret Abstract for week ending January 15, 1938, entitled 'Hindu Affairs' and 'Summary report of the meeting held in the Tilak Smarak Mandir on behalf of Poona Students', August 3, 1937; Maharashtra State Archives (MSA), Home Special Dept. 60 D (g) Pt. III, 1938, 'Extract from the Bombay Province weekly letter No. 31, dated August 5, 1939; MSA, Home Special Department, 1009 III 1942, police report entitled 'A summary report of the concluding ceremony of the Officers' Training Camp of the Rashtriya Swayam Sewak Sangh, at Poona on the May 27, 1943' and note from the Home Department Special, dated June 10, 1943.

40 *Towards Freedom: Documents on the Movement for Independence in India 1943-1944, Part III,* edited by Partha Sarathi Gupta, Indian Council for Historical Research, Oxford University Press, 1997.

41 Ibid., p. 3041.

42 Ibid., p. 3066.

43 Ibid., pp. 3047–48, 50, 51.

44 Nicholas Mansergh, *The Transfer of Power 1942–1947,* H.M. S.O., London, Vol. IV, p. 1123.

45 *Historic Statements,* V.D. Savarkar, pp. 109–13.

46 Ibid., pp. 219–20.

47 Ibid., p. 216.

## 5 Gandhi's murder

1 The Rashtriya Swayam Sevak Sangh, *Economic and Political Weekly,* Part III of the Article March 25, 1972, p. 681 Andersen came to India over three decades ago. He is now a respected 'India hand' at the U.S. State Department.

2 Keer, *Savarkar and His Times,* 1950, p. 371.

3 See Gauba, pp. 376–77 for the text.

4 Kapur Report, Part II, pp. 44–47.

5 Jagdish Chandra Jain, *I Could Not Save Bapu,* Jagran Sahitya Mandir, Kamacha, Benares, 1949.

6 Chief Ministers were called Prime Minister under the Government of India Act, 1935.

7 Kapur Report, Part II, p. 356, paragraphs 26, 112, 113 and 114.

8 See Chapter I, p. 40.

9 See Chapter I, p. 43, for the reference.

10 Darga Das (ed.) *Sardar Patel's Correspondence 1945–50,* Navjivan Publishing House, Ahmedabad, 1973, vol. 6, p. 63.

11 Ibid., p. 65.

12 Kapur Report, Part II, p. 303, paragraph 2, p. 106.

13 Gopal Godse, *May it please Your Honour: Statement of Nathuram Godse,*

Pune, 1977, p. 4. Subsequent references to this book are in the main text.

[14] Payne, *Life and Death of Mahatma Gandhi*, p. 618.

[15] Paragraphs 7, 8 and 9 of Savarkar's statement in Court dated November 20, 1948, NAI. The National Archives of India in New Delhi hold the Printed Record of the Mahatma Gandhi Murder Case. The writer is indebted to the NAI for permission to consult it and for copies of parts of the Record.

[16] Gopal Godse, *Gandhi Ji's Murder And After*, translated into English by Prof. S.T. Godbole, Surya-Prakashan, Nai Sarak, Delhi 1989. Subsequent references in the main text.

[17] Keer, *Savarkar and his Times*, 1950, p. 368.

[18] Ibid., p. 369.

[19] Collins and Lapierre, *Freedom at Midnight*, p. 364.

[20] Ibid., pp. 383–84.

[21] P.L. Inamdar, *The Story of the Red Fort Trial 1948–49*, Popular Prakashan, Bombay, 1979, p. 141.

[22] Ibid., p. 142.

[23] Ibid., p. 143.

[24] Kapur Report, Part II, pp. 37–70.

[25] Keer, *Veer Savarkar*, 1966, p. 477.

[26] See evidence of prosecution witness Seth Charandas Meghaji.

[27] See PW 86, p. 418.

[28] See *Gandhi Murder Trial*, Tagore Memorial Publications, New Delhi, 1949 for the text besides the authoritative text in the National Archives of India, New Delhi.

[29] Kapur Report, Part II, p. 300, paragraphs 25.92 and 25.93.

[30] Ibid., Part II, p. 303, paragraph 25.106.

[31] Ibid., p. 305, paragraph 25.113.

[32] Ibid., Part I, p. 36, paragraph 3.58.

[33] Ibid., p. 54, paragraph 19.18.

[34] Ibid., p. 59, paragraph 19.45.

[35] Kapur Report, Part II, p. 74.

[36] Chandrachud Report, pp. 7–8.

[37] Collins and Lapierre, *Freedom at Midnight*, p. 362.

[38] Ibid., p. 453.

## 6 The aftermath

[1] S. Gopal (ed.), *Selected Works of Jawaharlal Nehru*, Jawaharlal Nehru Memorial Fund, Oxford University Press, Second Series, vol. 5, p. 52.

[2] Darga Das (ed.), *Sardar Patel's Correspondence 1945–50*, Navjivan Publishing House, Ahmedabad, 1973, vol. 6, p. 66

3 *International Herald Tribune*, October 15, 2002.
4 See Noorani, *The RSS and the BJP*, p. 31.
5 Keer, *Veer Savarkar*, pp. 430–31.
6 Ibid., p. 432.
7 Savarkar, *Historic Statements*, p. 235.
8 Ibid., p. 224.
9 Keer, *Veer Savarkar*, p. 527.
10 Payne, *The Life and Death of Mahatma Gandhi*, p. 209.
11 *The Times of India*, November 22, 1993.
12 Interview with Gopal Godse by Arvind Rajagopal, *Frontline*, January 28, 1994.

# BIBLIOGRAPHY


1970. *Report of Commission of Inquiry into Conspiracy to Murder Mahatma Gandhi,* New Delhi,

1970. *Report Regarding the Facts and Circumstances Relating to the Death of Shri Deen Dayal Upadhyaya,* New Delhi, Government of India Press

Ambedkar, B.R., 1946. *Pakistan or Partition of India,* Bombay, Thacker & Co. Ltd, Third Edition

Andersen, Walter K. and Shridhar D. Damle, 1987. *The Brotherhood in Saffron,* New Delhi, Vistaar

Andersen, Walter K., 1972. 'The Rashtriya Swayam Sewak Sangh', *Economic and Political Weekly,* March 25

Casolari, Marzia, 2000. 'Hindutva's Foreign Tie-up in the 1930's: Archival Evidence', *Economic and Political Weekly,* January 22

Chandra, Bipan, 1984. *Communalism in Modern India,* Vikas

Chaterji, Joya, 1995. *Bengal Divided, Hindu Communalism and Partition,* Cambridge University Press

Collins, Larry and Dominique Lapierre, 1976. *Freedom at Midnight,* Vikas

*Constituent Assembly Debates,* volume IV

Das, Darga (ed.), 1973. *Sardar Patel's Correspondence 1945–50,* volume 6, Ahmedabad, Navjivan Publishing House

Dasgupta, Swapan, 1993. 'Nationhood Specified: Hindutva as a Double-Edged Sword', *The Times of India,* June 9

*Debates of the Legislative Council of Bombay,* volume 14, part 10

Dixit, Prabha, 1974. *Communalism: A Struggle for Power,* Orient Longman

Dubey, Krishnan and Venkitesh Ramakrishnan, 1995.'Far from heroism: The tale of "Veer Savarkar"', *Frontline,* April 7

Godse, Gopal, 1977. *May it please Your Honour: Statement of Nathuram Godse,* Pune

Godse, Gopal, 1989. *Gandhi Ji's Murder And After,* translated into English by Prof. Godbole, S.T., Delhi, Surya-Prakashan

Golwalkar, 1968. *Bunch of Thoughts,* Bangalore, Vikrama Prakashan

Gopal, Sarvepalli (ed.). *Selected Works of Jawaharlal Nehru,* volume 5, Oxford

University Press, Second Series

Gopal, Sarvepalli, 1991, *Anatomy of a Confrontation: The Babri Masjid–Ram Janmabhoomi Issue,*

Hasan, Mushirul (ed.), 1992. *Islam and Indian Nationalism: Reflections on Abdul Kalam Azad,* Manohar

Hasan, Mushirul, 2002. 'Text books and Imagined History: The BJP's Intellectual Agenda', *India International Centre Quarterly,* Summer

Inamdar, P.L., 1979. *The Story of the Red Fort Trial 1948–49,* Bombay, Popular Prakashan

Intelligence Bureau, *Terrorism in India (1917–1936)*

Jain, Jagdish Chandra, 1949. *I Could Not Save Bapu,* Benares, Jagran Sahitya Mandir

Jayakar, M.R., 1958. *The Story of My Life,* Asia Publishing House

Keegan, John, 1999. *The First World War,* New York, Alfred A. Knopf

Keer, Dhananjay, 1950. *Savarkar and His Times*

Keer, Dhananjay, 1966. *Veer Savarkar,* Bombay, Popular Prakashan

Majumdar, R.C. (general editor) and A.K. Majumdar (asstistant editor), 1969. *Struggle for Freedom,* Mumbai, Bhartiya Vidya Bhavan

Majumdar, R.C., 1975. *Penal Settlements in Andamans,* New Delhi, Gazetters Unit, Government of India

Mansergh, Nicholas. *The Transfer of Power 1942–1947,* volume IV, London, H.M. S.O.

Mehta, Asoka, 1946. *1857: A Great Rebellion,* Bombay, Hind Kitabs

Mishra, B.B., 1976. *The Indian Political Parties,* OUP

Mookerjee, Shyama Prasad, 1993. *Leaves from a Diary,* OUP

Mukherjee, Rudrangshu (ed.), 1993. *The Penguin Gandhi Reader,* Penguin Books

Munshi, K.M. 1967. *Indian Constitutional Documents,* volume 1, Bharatiya Vidya Bhawan

Munshi, K.M., 1967. *Pilgrimage to Freedom (1909–1950),* Bharatiya Vidya Bhawan

National Archives of India, 1949. *Gandhi Murder Trial,* New Delhi, Tagore Memorial Publications

Noorani, A.G., 1991. 'Legal Aspects to the Issue', in Gopal, 1991

Noorani, A.G., 2001. *The RSS and the BJP: A Division of Labour,* New Delhi, LeftWord Books, Second Edition

Noorani, A.G., 2001. *The Trial of Bhagat Singh: Politics of Justice,* Oxford University Press

Noorani, A.G., 2002. *Citizen's Rights, Judges and State Accountability,* Oxford University Press

Noorani, A.G., 2002. *Islam and Jihad,* New Delhi, LeftWord Books

Payne, Robert, 1969. *The Life and Death of Mahatma Gandhi,* The Bodley Head

Rajagopal, Arvind, 1994. Interview with Gopal Godse, *Frontline,* January 28

Savarkar, V.D. 1949. *Hindu Rashtra Darshan*, edited by L.G. Khare, Mumbai

Savarkar, V.D., 1950. *The Story of My Transportation of Life*, translated into English by V.N. Naik, Bombay, Sadbhakti Publications

Savarkar, V.D., 1967. *Historic Statements*, edited by S.S. Savarkar and G.M. Joshi, Mumbai, Popular Prakashan

Savarkar, V.D., 1969. *Hindutva: Who is a Hindu?*, S.S. Savarkar, Mumbai, Veer Savarkar Prakashan, Fifth Edition

Savarkar, V.D., 1970. *Six Glorious Epochs of Indian History*, New Delhi, Rajadhani Granthnagar

Savarkar, V.D., *An Echo from Andamans*

Sitaramayya, 1947, *The History of the Indian National Congress*, volume II (1935–1947), Bombay, Padma

Sunderam, Lanka, 1994. *Secular State for India: Thoughts on India's Political Future*, Delhi, Raj Kamal Publications

Swami, Praveen, 2000. *The Kargil War*, New Delhi, LeftWord Books

Vachha, P.B., 1962. *Famous Judges, Lawyers and Cases of Bombay: A Judicial History of Bombay During the British Period*, Bombay, N.M. Tripathi

# INDEX